Colonel Charles Dahnmon Whitt

Confederate American

Colonel Charles Dahnmon Whitt

ISBN 978-1-931672-70-2

Dahnmon Whitt Family in cooperation with
Jesse Stuart Foundation
Ashland Kentucky

First Edition January 17, 2011

Copyright 2010 by Colonel Charles Dahnmon Whitt
All rights reserved. NO part of this book may be reproduced or utilized in any form or by any means without the permission from the publisher.

Published by:

*Jesse Stuart Foundation
1645 Winchester Avenue, Ashland, Kentucky 41101
dahnmonwhittfamily.com*

Confederate American

Dedicated to:

The descendents of the Great Southern Army and Navy 1861-1865.

My late Great Grandfather David Crockett Whitt which served in the 29th Virginia Infantry. CSA

My late Father Marvin B. Whitt for his faith in me.

My Dear Wife, Sharon, for help and support in my writing efforts.

My Brothers, Jerry and Larry Whitt for support and other work.

Colonel Charles Dahnmon Whitt

Contents:

Chapter 1.	*Page 5*	Why A Confederate?
Chapter 2.	*Page 11*	Confederate's Food.
Chapter 3.	*Page 16*	Confederate Uniforms
Chapter 4.	*Page 21*	Confederate Weapons
Chapter 5.	*Page 33*	Confederates at Play.
Chapter 6.	*Page 39*	Marching and Transportation
Chapter 7	*Page 52*	A W O L
Chapter 8.	*Page 55*	Trade between Yank and Reb.
Chapter 9.	*Page 62*	Lee's Miserables, POW
Chapter 10	*Page 99*	Love for Lee and Jackson
Chapter 11	*Page 115*	Tricks of War
Chapter 12	*Page 121*	Black Confederates
Chapter 13	*Page 129*	Confederate Doctors
Chapter 14	*Page 141*	Rebel Yell
Chapter 15	*Page 151*	Flags of the Confederates
Chapter 16	*Page 161*	Songs of the Confederates
Chapter 17	*Page 190*	Women as Weapons
Chapter 18	*Page 201*	Economy of CSA
Chapter 19	*Page 218*	Confederates and God
Chapter 20	*Page 230*	Reconstruction
	Page 298	About the "Old Colonel"

Confederate American

A lost, but not forgotten, Nation.

Colonel Charles Dahnmon Whitt
Chapter 1
Why a Confederate?

I believe the number one reason the average Southern Man picked up a musket and joined the Confederacy was, "The North Invaded the South!"

Many things led up to the Civil War and I hope to touch on many of them.

Who were these citizen soldiers that held off the might of the United States for four grueling years? They were the farm boys, shop keepers, the adventurers, the dutiful, the rich and the poor. They were mere boys to old men. Some were brave and some joined to be counted with the brave. Some fought for honor, some fought for their state, and some fought for their land and family.

Most of the common Confederates were natural born soldiers. They, as a majority could ride, handle horses, shoot muskets and had a spirit that many of their counterparts from the North did not have.

They could survive and even flourish on common food fare. They were used to hard work and possessed many skills that would be beneficial in defending their homes. Most of the men from the South lived a rugged life as they were country folk and self-reliant.

Many of the Northern men were from bigger towns and cities and really did not have the zeal for a war with their southern countrymen.

Confederate American

The Confederate had the zeal and spirit because they felt they were defending their country. This is why the North could not put the South down for such a long time.

The Southern men had a different prospective on the word Country, than did the North. This was hard to overcome even back when the Southern States joined the Union in the first place.

The Southern Men looked upon their State as their Country. They put State first and United States second. When the North began raising an Army so did the South. The Confederates looked on the North as invaders and they were not going to stand by and let that happen. The Confederates looked at the new war as the second Revolution.

Was it over slaves, as many think today? Just let me give you a few little known facts and you can draw your own conclusion. Only 2% of the Confederate solders owned slaves. The slave owners were the rich and by the time the war came the concentration of slaves were in the Deep South on the cotton plantations.

Did you know that General Grant's wife owned slaves while he led the Northern Army?

Did you know that Abraham Lincoln made the statement that he would free no slaves, free some slave, or free all slaves if it would preserve the Union? When Lincoln had to make a move to make the war more popular, he waited for some semblance of a battle victory. After the battle of Antietam Lincoln proclaimed that the slaves in the Confederate States were free. Notice that he never freed the slaves in the North. *Bet you didn't know that!*

Colonel Charles Dahnmon Whitt

When the war became highly unpopular in the North, Lincoln used the cause of slavery as a means to gain support for the war. The people had riots in the street of the bigger cities during this time so Lincoln had to do something.

General Lee and the South thought if they held on, Lincoln would lose the election for his second term and the South would be left alone to form their own southern country.

Why did he not free them in the North? That would be political suicide. The northerners that owned slaves began to call their slaves, "Servants"! They began to cover up the fact that their servants could not leave. Some were freed, and some were sold or given away. Of course the slave owners in the North were not as numerous as their counterparts in the South.

What about the right to secede? I want to give a little explanation as to the thinking of the southern folks.

The first union of the original 13 colonies was affected by the Articles of Confederation, adopted in 1781. The Articles established a confederation of sovereign states in a permanent union. The *"permanence"* lasted until 1788, when 11 states withdrew from the confederation and ratified the new Constitution, which became effective on March 4, 1789. The founding fathers recognized the defects in the Articles of Confederation, learned from those defects, and scrapped the articles in favor of the "more perfect union" found in the Constitution.

Nowhere in the Constitution is there any mention of the states being permanent. This was not an oversight by any means. Indeed, when New York, Rhode Island, and Virginia ratified the Constitution, they specifically stated that

Confederate American

they reserved the right to resume the governmental powers granted by the United States. Their claim to the right of secession was understood and agreed to by the ratifiers, including George Washington, who presided over the Constitutional Convention and was a delegate from Virginia.

A book, *"Life of Webster"* by Henry Cabot Lodge stated "It is safe to say that there was not a man in the country, from Washington and Hamilton to Clinton and Mason, who did not regard the new system as an experiment from which every State had a right to peaceable withdraw."

A text book used at West Point before the Civil War, "A View of the Constitution," written by Judge William Rawle, states; *"The secession of a State depends on the will of the people of such a State."*

In other words, if a State didn't like being in the Union as explained by the new Constitution of the United States, that State could just quit and be it's own country.

The differences of the Northern States to the Southern States had been a problem from the beginning of the new Union of the Independent States called the United States of America.

Colonel Charles Dahnmon Whitt

This is the Battle Flag of the Confederacy. It had two extra stars, one for Maryland and one for Kentucky which never officially join the Confederacy.

Confederate American

The Southern States especially felt that their State was an Independent Nation and did not have to answer to any other body as to how they governed themselves.

The one thing I want you to know and remember is that the word, *"Confederate,"* is not a dirty word and many men died trying to defend their homes.

I hope to educate folks about the War Between the States. Why it came to pass and why it never has been completely settled.

General Lee instructs Colonel Whitt at the Re-enactment of Jeffersonville Skirmish in April 2010

Colonel Charles Dahnmon Whitt
Chapter 2
Confederate's Food

The Confederates ate pretty well the first year of the war, but both quality and quantity diminished as the war went on. Of course the Confederates had some foods that the North did not and the North had some the South did not. The North had access to imported foods and other materials as the Confederates did not. The South had to raise their foods or capture it from the North because of the Northern Blockade all around the Southern sea ports.

You must remember that they had no refrigeration in the 1860's. They either had to have their foods dried, pickled, salted, or they had to eat it in season. Salt was in big demand as the main preservative. This made Saltville in southwest Virginia and Leatherwood, Kentucky prime targets for the North because of their salt works.

The main bread of the North was "Hardtack," and for the South was "Johnny Cakes." These breads were kept for days and often became infested with weevils and or all manner of germs.

The Civil War food may have kept the average soldier fed and not much else. The Commissary Departments were to gather the foods and distribute them the best ways as possible. The seasons of the year determined what types of food that might be available.

The North had an advantage or two over the Confederates. The North had an existing Commissary Department that was trained in how to acquire large quantities of food, preserve it and get it to the troops, whereas the Confederates had to learn. The other

Confederate American

advantage the North held was that the coast of the South was blockaded and imports could not come in.

The South being mindful of each state's rights became a hindrance in some cases. The railroad track spacing in one state sometimes did not match those in another state. They all did not adopt the 4' 8 ½" standard gage. This would lead to time loss as one train would have to be unloaded at the state line and another train loaded to advance the supplies to the troops.

The Confederate had to be dedicated and fight many times on an empty stomach. Many times the Confederates would capture supplies from the North, but if they were pushed back the Confederates would have to go foraging around the country side just to be able to eat. While marching to Gettysburg they ate the green corn they came upon. This often caused many trips behind a bush!

When the Commissary did come through it was mostly simple fare such as salt pork, hardtack, fruits or vegetables in season if they could get them.

The soldiers carried haversacks with some food and personal items with them when they were in the field. The "Haversacks" were canvass or in some cases leather bags with a strap that went over the shoulder. The haversacks were sometimes tarred on the outside to keep them water proofed. They usually had a cloth lining that could be taken out and washed. Sometimes the haversacks could become quiet smelly as food became bad. Beef jerky, Johnny cakes and parched corn could be eaten on the march.

Colonel Charles Dahnmon Whitt

The North typically had coffee and tea, but not much tobacco for their pipes. The Confederates had tobacco to smoke after a meal, but not any coffee or tea as the war progressed. This would bring on trade meetings between Confederates and Yankees on picket duty between battles. The both Armies forbid such meetings, but men will be men.

In good times the Confederate had some salt bacon, corn meal, tea, sugar, molasses, and a fresh vegetable. Many times the vegetable would be sweet potatoes.

There was a story handed down by word of mouth that came to me by my late father, Marvin Whitt. I think it came down from his grandfather David Crockett Whitt which served with the twenty-ninth Virginia Infantry. He said, "Some Yankee spies were out watching the Confederates gather food. To the shock of the Yankees the Confederates were digging roots close to a poplar grove and it appeared to them that the Confederates were planning to eat poplar roots. The Yankees hurried back to their command and gave the report," "Ain't no way we can beat these southerners, they are digging poplar roots and eating them!"

The main food of the Confederate was "Coosh"! It was made from his rations of a small piece of salt pork, often too small to cook alone. The meat was fried rendering out mostly hog fat, then flour was added, then milk or water was poured into the hot grease while stirring rapidly. The dirty brown mess was ready to eat. It was "gravy like" substance. The Confederates liked it because it was filling and lasted for a while.

Sometimes near a large town the women folks would bake big loafs of white bread and bring it to the soldiers, but the

Confederate American

white bread didn't hold back hunger as long as their "Coosh."

The officers always tried to get their men Kraut or fresh cabbage as it proved to hold back the dreaded "Scurvy" (A lack of vitamin "C")

In the trenches at Petersburg during the winter of 1864 and 1865 the Confederates subsisted on frozen cabbage as that is about all they could get!

It is said that an army, *"Fights on its stomach!"* The Confederates fought on their spirit and said little of their condition. They may have reflected on their forefathers at Valley Forge and compare themselves to the first Revolutionary War. They felt *"Freedom,"* was more important than worrying over what they had or did not have to eat. One thing for sure, the average Confederate was thin.

Colonel Charles Dahnmon Whitt

Re-enactors marching, but look at the diversity of uniforms.

Confederate American

Chapter 3
Confederate Uniforms

To put it plainly, they wore a great assortment of clothes, colors, and styles. Some men fought throughout the war with never having a uniform.

The Confederates had a list of clothing that was to be issued to each man, but this was never really accomplished. It was more like a dream sheet, but some units did get most of the items on the list.

Clothing Allowance:		Number
Cap or Hat	$2.00	1 or 2
Jacket	$12.00	1
Trousers	$9.00	1
Shirt	$3.00	2 or 3
Drawers	$3.00	2 or 3
Shoes	$6.00	4
Socks	$1.00	4
Leather stock	$0.25	0 to 1
Great Coat	$25.00	0 to 1
Fatigue overall Blanket	$7.50	1

One major problem was getting uniforms and supplies to the armies in the field. It is ironic, but time caught up with the soldiers and in the last six months of the war, the Army of Northern Virginia was issued 104,199 jackets, 157,727 cotton shirts, 74,851 blankets, 140,570 pairs of trousers, 170,139 pairs of drawers, (Long drawers were really important, they shielded the solders from contact with the irritating wool.) 27,011 hats and caps, 4,861 great coats, 167,862 pairs of shoes, and 21,063 pairs of shoes.

Colonel Charles Dahnmon Whitt

I was surprised at this list, because up to this period the men were poorly equipped. Food was still a dire need during these last six months. (This information came from Leslie D. Jensen.)

Some states tried to take care of their own soldiers, the central government tried to help and some units were supplied by private sources and even family. The militia was called up near Bristol at the beginning of the war. Private John Singleton Mosby was part of this group. The men were issued prison uniforms, but they refused them and wore their personal clothes until some better uniforms were issued. Private Mosby advanced to Colonel before the war ended and became the famous "Gray Ghost!"

Most of the Confederate uniforms were made of wool and were some shade of gray to butternut brown. The uniforms were made out of any color they could get but they tried to keep them a shade of gray. The uniforms mostly copied those of the Union Army in style.

Wool was very durable but also very hot in summer. A lot of both Union and Confederate solders suffered heat strokes on long summer marches.

This reminds me of the frequent "Skinny Dipping" sessions the Confederates enjoyed. There was a woman soldier that belonged to such a group but no one new she was a woman. She never went swimming with the men, but enjoyed sitting on the bank and watching the naked men frolic in the water.

There was one account that a unit of Confederates was surprised by oncoming Yankees and they came out of the water, grabbed their muskets, and fought naked.

Confederate American

The Confederates earned the name of "Ragged Rebel" because of their appearance they gave marching through the countryside. The Confederates were described as dirty, greasy, and tattered but they didn't mind as long as General Lee and other leaders gave them victories over the well dressed Union Army.

One Lady in Maryland observed the Confederates marching through her state and exclaimed, *"Is this ragged bunch of scarecrows what's been beating our boys?"*

The ragged Southern Army looked unbeatable and triumphant after winning a battle over their foes, but didn't look too bad if they lost.

The Confederates often picked up supplies and materials after a battle they had won. The shoes were a hot item to take from a fallen Yankee. By the end of the war some Confederates looked more Yankee that Rebel. (Lee's Army of Northern Virginia seemed to be an exception, as they received uniform items late in the war.) They wore the blue pants and sometimes even the blue coats because that was all they had.

Colonel Charles Dahnmon Whitt

Young private Edwin Francis Jemison, killed 1862
One of the better dressed Confederates.
Look how young he looks.

Confederate American

This is three typical, proud, but slim Confederates. Notice the differences in their uniforms. They are thought to be captured.
"I dare you; capture me!"

Colonel Charles Dahnmon Whitt

Chapter 4
Confederate Weapon's

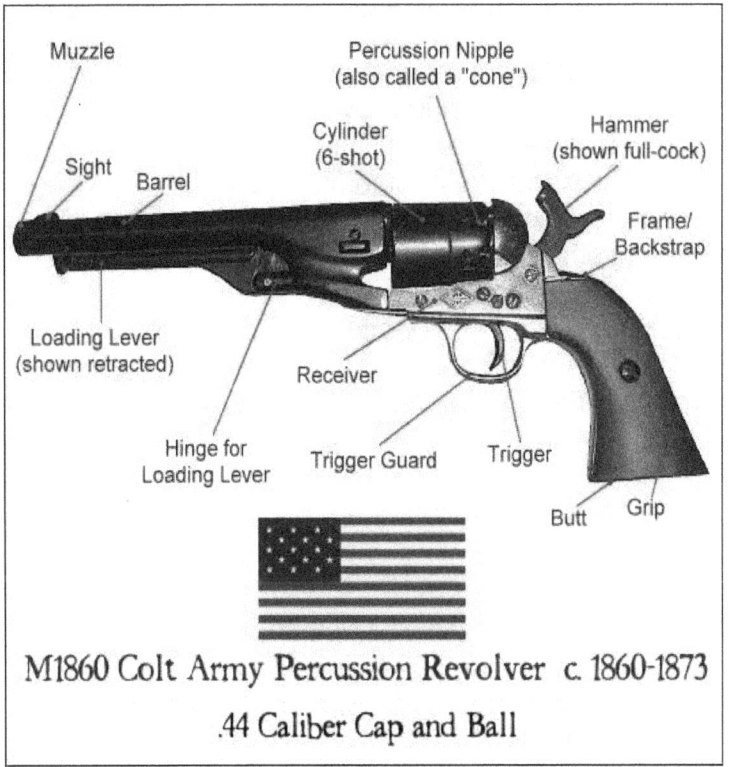

M1860 Colt Army Percussion Revolver c. 1860-1873
.44 Caliber Cap and Ball

This piece was made in the north, but the south had their version.

Confederate American

Once again the south as well as the north was quite diverse in its weapons. Inventions for killing their fellowman spring up like mushrooms. The Industrial Revolution brought on many inventions and ways of manufacturing. The North was far ahead of the South in manufacturing all things, especially war materials.

The standard musket for the Confederate Infantry was the .577 caliber British Enfield 1853 smooth bore rifled musket. This musket was reliable, quick loading and very accurate. The Confederates started out with the old smooth bore .69 caliber converted flintlocks. The percussion cap was a great improvement over flintlock as you could use it in wet weather. The south started out with whatever muskets they could come up with. They had the .32 caliber squirrel guns, shotguns, and even the muzzle loading single shots from the war of 1812.

Revolver pistols or shot guns became popular with the Calvary. Colonel John S. Mosby said, *"It is much easier to ride up and shoot the enemy, than to whack at them with a sword."*

After Colonel Mosby became a leader in the hit and run Calvary of the Confederacy, he made it his plan to arm each man with a six shot revolver. (They were black powder, no cartridge type.) Many of the Confederate Calvary carried muzzle loading shotguns which worked well in close combat. When a shotgun was brought from home, it could be either a single or a double barrel. It could and did fire either shot, or a single large round ball, and sometimes both at once if the cavalryman who loaded it could stand the recoil. If the round ball with a cloth patch was a reasonably snug fit, it could be as accurate

Colonel Charles Dahnmon Whitt

out to a hundred yards or so as the sights or the shooter's skill allowed. "Ram and fire fast" is a descriptive term of the Confederate cavalry racing with their shotguns to beat the Federals to the next crossing across the Rappahannock River.

The Confederates had many weapons.
The Union had better weapons. Notice the old single shot flint lock pistol.

Confederate American

Sharon Gail my Southern Bell, Yes women were used as Weapons!

Colonel Charles Dahnmon Whitt

The .58 caliber Enfield was the preferred musket of both armies. It fired the accurate "Minnie Ball." Below is the bayonet that fits this musket.

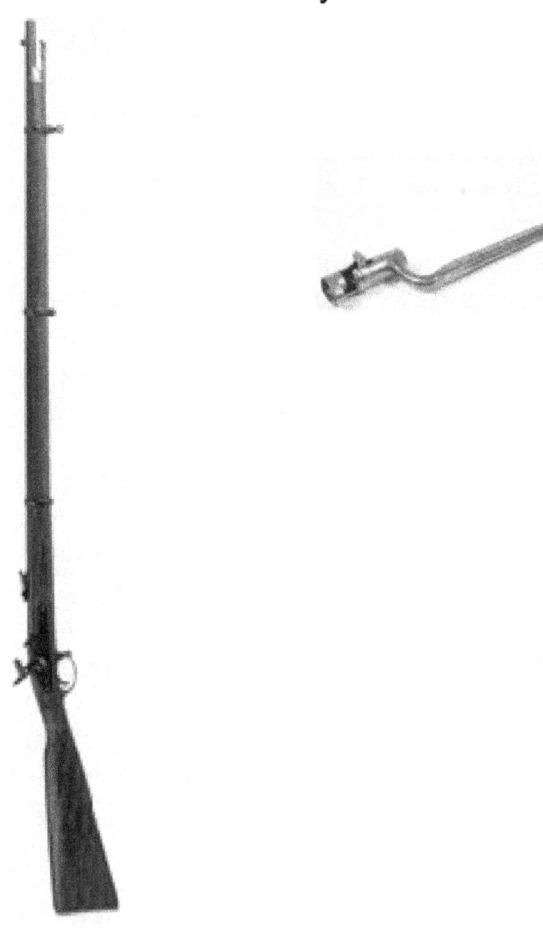

Confederate American

The South was always out to capture weapons and supplies. To capture cannon that had been fired on them was a win in itself. To turn that cannon toward the retreating Yankees was wonderful indeed.

To push back Union troops while they cooked breakfast was a wonderful gift. The Confederates would just sit down and eat the Yankee's breakfast. This happened more than once. At Chancellorsville the Rebels got the Yankee's supper when General Jackson flanked the unsuspecting Union Army of General Hooker.

All firearms larger than small arms are known as artillery or cannon. Although there were dozens of different types of cannon used during the Civil War, they all fell into one of two categories: smoothbore or rifled cannon. They were further designated by the weight of their projectile (12-pounder, 24-pounder, 32-pounder, etc.), the caliber or size of their bore diameter (3-inch, 8-inch, 10-inch), method of loading (breech or muzzle), and often their inventor or the factory in which they were made (i.e. Dahlgren, Napoleon, Rodman, Parrott, Whitworth). A further distinction involved the path of their trajectories: guns had a flat trajectory, mortars a high, arching path, and a howitzer a trajectory between the other two. Civil War artillery was also classified according to its tactical deployment, including field, seacoast, and siege artillery. Cannons were made of steel, bronze, or iron, depending on the availability of material.

The favorite artillery piece in both the Union and the Confederacy was the Napoleon, a smoothbore, muzzle-loading, 12-pounder *"gun-howitzer."* Developed under the auspices of Louis Napoleon of France, it first appeared in

Colonel Charles Dahnmon Whitt

the American artillery in 1857. Relatively light and portable, the Napoleon was used as both an offensive and defensive weapon by both armies. Initially made of bronze, Napoleons were cast from iron when the South ran short of the other metal. Its maximum effective range was about 1,700 yards, but it was most effective at about 250 yards or less. Firing canister (see below), the Napoleon probably inflicted more casualties than all other artillery pieces combined.

The most used rifled guns were the 3-inch Ordinance and 10-pdr Parrott rifles. These cannon were more accurate and had a longer range; up to about 2,300 yards - than their smoothbore counterparts. During most battles, however, the longer range was unnecessary and relatively ineffective. During this period, a gunner had to see his target in order to shoot with any accuracy and the shorter range Napoleons were adequate for that purpose.

However, rifled cannons were particularly effective in knocking down fortifications and played decisive roles at Vicksburg and Atlanta. Almost all Civil War cannon were muzzle loading models, such as the British 12-pounder rifled Armstrong and Whitworth cannons were generally unreliable and awkward. The 12-pound mountain howitzers were among the smallest and most portable artillery and were useful in battles fought in the mountainous regions of the Western theater. Naval and siege cannons, including Dahlgrens and Rodman smoothbores, were among the heaviest and most powerful. The 8- and 10-inch siege howitzers had ranges of over 2,000 yards and could fire 45 and 90pound shells. Artillery ammunition included solid shot, grape, canister, shell, and chain shot, each of which came in any of the nine common artillery calibers. Solid shot and shell were used against long-range, fixed targets such as

Confederate American

fortifications, chain shot, consisting of two balls connected by a chain, was used primarily against masts and rigging of ships. This took some experimentation and loss of heads and limbs to perfect.

Very frequently used was canister which, like its larger cousin, "grape shot," was a scattershot projectile consisting of small iron balls encased in a container. Canister projectiles came packed in a tin can while grape shot was usually wrapped in a cloth or canvas covering and tied with string which made it look like a bunch of grapes. When fired, the can or wrapping disintegrated, releasing the shot in a spray. In effect, then, a gun loaded with grape shot or canister acted like a large, sawed-off shotgun; it was particularly lethal when fired at a range of 250 yards or less. Grape was less often used by the field artilleries of the day as it was more effective to fire the smaller and more numerous canister balls at an advancing enemy. Thanks to its superior industrial strength, the North had an overall advantage over the South in all types of artillery, as well as a higher percentage of rifled cannon to smoothbore cannon.

The development of this half-inch lead rifle bullet revolutionized warfare, while the slowness of Civil War military leaders to adapt their tactics to adjust to the new technology was greatly responsible for the overwhelming number of battlefield deaths.

Before the introduction of what soldiers commonly called the *"Minie Ball,"* (Named for the inventor, not because of size.) Even though it was indeed bullet shaped, the use of rifles in battle was impractical and largely limited to corps of elite marksmen. Expensive, tight fitting projectiles had

Colonel Charles Dahnmon Whitt

to be jammed into the grooves of the rifle's muzzle, a time-consuming process.

In 1848, however, French army Captain Claude F. Minie created a smaller, hollow-based bullet that could far more quickly and easily be rammed into the bore, expanding when the weapon was fired to catch in the rifling and be shot spinning out of the barrel. That spin made the Minie ball like other, more expensive and unwieldy rifle bullets, a highly precise and far traveling projectile. They could reach a half a mile or more and an average soldier could easily hit a target 250 yards away.

By 1855, Harpers Ferry Armory worker James H. Burton had honed an even cheaper version of the Minie ball, which, along with the rifle itself, soon became widely used in the U.S. Army. It was the standard bullet for both sides in the Civil War, although neither anticipated the enormous difference this would make on the battlefield. An army charging a defensive line using musket fire- requiring a 25-second reloading period and accurate to only 50 feet or less. A frontal infantry charge was likely to be successful if the assaulting force moved quickly enough.

The widespread use of the Minie Ball bullet, however, shifted the balance greatly to the defense's favor. Nevertheless, Civil War generals continued ordering such attacks, learning only after hard and bloody battlefield experience. The assault on Marye's Heights at Fredericksburg and Pickett's Charge at Gettysburg made them change their strategy.

Confederate American

Swords, Sabers, Knifes, and even Lances

Bayonets, sabers, swords, short swords, cutlasses, Bowie knives, pikes, and lances, classified as *"edged weapons,"* appeared in considerable profusion during the Civil War. Although they served to decorate their original possessors and delight modern collectors, they inflicted few casualties. In *"Regimental Losses,"* Fox points out that of the approximately 250,000 wounded treated in Union hospitals during the war only 922 were the victims of sabers or bayonets. *"And a large proportion of these originated in private quarrels or was inflicted by camp guards in the discharge of their duty."* A few instances of bayonet attacks are recorded. Among the few recorded instances are the charge of the 17th Wisconsin at Corinth, Mississippi, 3 Oct. 1862, routing a Mississippi brigade; and the night bayonet attack of the 6th Maine and 5th Wisconsin at Rappahonnock Bridge and Kelly's Ford, Va. 7 Nov. 1863.

Sabers, which are cavalry swords, are a legitimate weapon of the mounted service and dangerous in the hands of a trained trooper. The volunteer horsemen, however, had trouble learning to handle them. There were a good many lop-eared horses (poor things) in the early months of the war. Gigantic *"wrist breakers"* with 42-inch scimitar-type blades were soon cut down to 36 inches and were reasonably effective.

Swords until recent years in America were the symbol of an officer's authority, and served this primary function in

Colonel Charles Dahnmon Whitt

the Civil War. The short artillery sword with which the gunners were supposed to disembowel the horse that had overrun their position and then dispatch the rider was among the most useless of weapons

The lance, another serious weapon in the hands of a trained trooper, also appeared in the war. The 6th Pennsylvania Calvary, *"Rush's Lancers,"* was armed with this weapon, in addition to its pistols and a few carbines, until May '63. The weapons shortage in the South led its leaders to give serious consideration to arming troops with lances and pikes. In early 1862 a set of resolutions provided for 20 regiments of Southern Pikemen and on 10 Apr. 1862 an act was passed that two companies in each regiment be armed with pikes. Strangely enough, such foolishness met with the complete approval of the military leaders, and even General Lee on April 9, 1862, wrote Col. Gorgas (Chief of Confederate Ordinance),

"One thousand pikes should be sent to General Jackson if practicable." Georgia's governor spurred the production of weapons that are now known as "JOE BROWN'S PIKES."

As Commander-in-Chief of the Georgia Militia, Governor Joseph E. Brown took emergency action to arm his troops. He put the shops in the State to work making what came to be known as "Joe Brown's Pikes." In his book *"Reminiscences of the Civil War,"* General John B. Gordon described the pike as "a sort of rude bayonet or steel lance fastened not to guns, but to long poles or handles, and were given to men who had no other arms." Many different forms of military cutlery, known generically as Bowie Knives, were popular among Confederate soldiers until discarded after real campaigning started.

Confederate American

Sources: The Civil War Society's "Encyclopedia of the Civil War and Mark M. Boatner's "Civil War Dictionary."

The South was the first to use the Submarine, Both sides had Iron Clad Ships, and both had hand grenades. Railroads and trains were even used as weapons. They had exploding bullets, but both sides decided not to use them. It was said, *"It's bad enough to shoot a feller, let alone blow him up!"*

Colonel Charles Dahnmon Whitt

Chapter 5

The Confederates at Play.

The Great snowball fight, Taken from the book, "The Army of Robert E. Lee," by Philip Katcher

Confederate American

"The parade ground has been a busy place for a week or so past, ball-playing having become a mania in camp. Officer and men forget, for a time, the differences in rank and indulge in the invigorating sport with a school boy's ardor."

Union Baseball Team.

Colonel Charles Dahnmon Whitt

The game of baseball was accepted and embraced by both the Confederates and the Union. The officers and men played together like boys to relieve the stresses of war.

"I see great things in baseball. It's our game - the American game. It will take our people out-of-doors, fill them with oxygen, give them a larger physical stoicism. Tend to relieve us from being a nervous, dyspeptic set. Repair these losses and be a blessing to us."

Walt Whitman
1846

Soldiers played all kinds of card games, chess and checkers, backgammon, dominoes, they read newspapers and books, played horseshoes, and they told stories. They also played whole team sports such as baseball and a very early often-brutal version of football.

Holidays in camp were cause for large celebrations. There were foot races, feasts, horse races, music shows, and all types of different contests that were put on by the troops.

Basically soldiers on both sides did anything they could to stop the boredom they often had to endure living in camp. Now of course all of these activities could never take place when an army was on an active campaign, during a campaign leisure time was relegated to basically writing letters, sleeping and keeping your equipment in working order. Smoking and chewing tobacco was enjoyed by the Southern Boys as well as a good drink of spirits when it

Confederate American

was around. They did miss their coffee, as the blockade stopped its import.

Another thing the Confederates loved, as time permitted, was to cook something special. That is, when food was available.

After the great victory at Fredericksburg, the snows came in and the Confederates had another battle amongst themselves!
This battle was known as the *"Great Snowball Battle of*

Gen. Robt. F. Hoke, North Carolina

Rappahannock Academy," this snowball fight started when back to back-to-back snowstorms, February 19th and 21st, 1863, delivered a one-two punch culminating in close to 17 inches on the ground, that covered the Confederate Army camped near Fredericksburg, Va.

Colonel Charles Dahnmon Whitt

Several days later, when the sun came out, the temperature became mild enough to soften the snow and the great assault by the "boys" of the youthful 26 year old General Robert F Hoke's North Carolinians upon the camp of their friendly rivals, the Georgians of Colonel Stiles Brigade began.

It was very similar to the real battles these veteran troops had participated in, the attacking force of the snow-ball army, led by officers, used cavalry, skirmishers and infantry in lines of battle as they pushed into the Georgians camp, and the "severe pelting" began. Hastily reinforced by soldiers from other camps, including even the cooks and teamsters, the Georgians were able to successfully repel the invaders. Georgia's Colonel William Stiles then held a "council of war," with his officers, determined to return the favor to the "Tar-heels" and capture their camp. Stiles organized his hundreds of Georgians into columns of companies, each man with a snowball in hand, and marched them into the enemy camp. Much to his chagrin, when they reached the Carolinians camp, he found his enemy had prepared and filled their haversacks to the brim with snowballs; giving them the ability to pelt the Georgians at will, without the need to 'reload'. Many Georgians were captured that day, and were "whitewashed," with snow as a punishment before being paroled (swearing an oath not to return to the fight) and released.

When all was said and done, nearly 10,000 Confederate soldiers had participated in this epic snowball battle. A few General officers witnessed the massive fight, including, it was said, Stonewall Jackson, who refused to participate.

Confederate American

There were a few minor injuries, as some of the less savory characters hurled snowball covered rocks, or chunks of ice. But for the most part it was all great fun for these young men, many of them who were truly still teenage boys. Unfortunately, so many of them would never make it home to retell the story of what one soldier called *"one of the most memorable combats of the war."*

(Source: Mike Radinsky, Maryland Civil War History Examiner.)

Winter of 1862 and 1863 near Fredericksburg

Colonel Charles Dahnmon Whitt
Chapter 6
Marching and Transportation

Marching and riding trains were about the only mode of transportation for the Confederate Infantry. According to the diary of Benjamin J. Huddle of the Twenty-ninth Virginia Infantry he covered some 6,561 miles during his time of the war. He rode trains some 3,249 miles and marched some 3,312 miles.

I would not try to undertake to estimate the miles of the Confederate Calvary as they traveled so much. The Calvary was the eyes and ears of the army. They were often the first to hit the enemy and often the rear guard in retreats.

The Confederates were spread thin trying to defend the south. Every hot spot that popped up would bring men from other areas in a hurry. The Confederates became very good at putting out the fires of battle by moving men around. One example of that was the battle of Saltville. They knew that the Yankees were coming out of Kentucky to destroy the salt works and wreak havoc on the southwestern Virginia countryside. Every able bodied man from a 150 mile circle, including men and boys, were rushed forward to slow the Union Army or get to Saltville, Virginia to make a stand.

Small groups of old men and boys gathered at Raven, Virginia (Before there was a Raven) where the Yankees were descending the Kentucky Turnpike down the steep ridge. About 300 hit the 8,000 Union soldiers and slowed them down. Then at the little town of Indian, (Now Cedar

Confederate American

Bluff, Virginia) another small party of old men with their squirrel guns and Old Betz muskets hit them again. This tactic worked and gave ample time for the more able bodied veterans to reach Saltville and fend off the Yankee's.

Confederate troops were often rushed to where they were needed most. This made it hard for the Union Army to ever get a handle on how many troops they faced.

After the Battle of Cold Harbor, the Confederates realized that Grant had moved on trying to find another way into Richmond. The Confederates were ordered to double-time march to face Grant's Blue Army again. They were not just ordered to double-time, but to trot like horses.

In the spring of 1863 and early summer, General Lee started to call his army together to make a run on the North. General Pickett's Division was making siege against the Yankees in Suffolk, Virginia. He waited until evening and built many camp fires and marched his men to the west. On May 3rd. they started a march and by May 4th they crossed the Blackwater River and made camp in south Hampton County.

General Pickett's Division had marched twenty-eight miles! Many men had bloody feet after that. The stragglers were left behind and captured by the Yankees. I can not imagine marching 28 miles in a week, let alone in one long night. You must remember the Confederates did not have the best of shoes and equipment, if they even had shoes. They were carrying a ten pound musket and what ever equipment they owned. Only their spirit and

Colonel Charles Dahnmon Whitt

will to defend their homeland enabled them to make such marches.

The trains played a big part in moving troops around, but as the war wore on the condition of the tracks and engines deteriorated. That's not counting the havoc the Yankees caused by tearing up the tracks every time they could.

Trains of the Civil War 1861-1865

Confederate American

The Civil War is renowned for the introduction and employment of many new weapons, including rifled artillery, machine guns, and submarines. To this list should also be added railroad weapons, which were the predecessors of modern armored fighting vehicles.

During the war, railroads were second only to waterways in providing logistical support for the armies. They were also vital to the economies of the divided nation. A great deal has been written about railroads in the war, and in particular the spectacular engineering feats of the U.S. Military Railroads' Construction Corps under Herman Haupt. But strangely, the tactical employment of locomotives and rolling stock, which was actually quite widespread, has thus far escaped serious attention.

Large military forces were, of course, the worst danger to railroads. Because they supplied the units that were on campaign, railroads were often major objectives of an army. Without supplies the Confederates could not operate for long. Since the only sure way to deal with large scale threats was with a force of similar size, armies often stayed near the railroad tracks. While armies campaigned, locomotives and rolling stock provided logistical support and some also performed tactical missions. These missions included close combat especially when the situation was fluid or when the railroad provided a convenient avenue of approach to an opponent.

In such situations commanders sometimes sent locomotives to reconnoiter the terrain and gain information on enemy troop dispositions. While this may seem like a risky venture gathering information was often worth the

Colonel Charles Dahnmon Whitt

risk and lone locomotives could quickly reverse direction and move as fast as 60 mph, far faster than pursuing cavalry. With such great mobility, locomotives were also useful as courier vehicles when commanders had to rush vital intelligence to headquarters. This communications service was an important advantage in a war where raiders frequently cut or tapped telegraph lines.

Useful as they were for tactical and logistical support locomotives were vulnerable to derailments and sharpshooters who might shoot a hole in a boiler or a crewman. Federal officers accordingly inspected rails and armored some of their engines against small-arms fire. Unfortunately, their crews found that the armor trapped too much heat inside the cabs and limited escape if there was an accident. This was an important consideration, since a burst boiler could scald a crew in their iron cab like lobsters in a pot. This grisly prospect encouraged many crewmen to take their chances by jumping from the cab in the event of a derailment. An eventual compromise included applying armor to some parts of the cab and installing small oval windows, thus reducing the chances of a sharpshooter's bullet penetrating the glass, while still letting the crew see where they were going.

In special situations, locomotives served as rams. Troops might start a locomotive down a track with a full head of steam to damage an enemy train or railroad facilities, or to attack troops. On one occasion, Confederate soldiers lurking near a burned bridge suddenly saw a burning ammunition train hurtling straight toward them, forcing them to run like rabbits. Troops sometimes launched individual cars, also set on fire, against the enemy or used them to burn bridges. The potential for such rolling threats prompted commanders to build obstructions on the tracks.

Confederate American

Freight trains might also deceive an enemy. A train might run back and forth into an area, tricking scouts into reporting that the enemy was reinforcing his position, when in fact he was leaving. One Confederate ruse involved sending an empty train down the tracks to entice hidden Yankee artillery into firing, thereby revealing their location.

While trains might serve as artillery bait, they could also transport heavy guns to the battlefield. Commanders took this idea a step further during the war by mounting heavy artillery pieces on flatcars for combat operations. Locomotives or manpower propelled these railroad batteries, dispensing with the horses that normally were the prime movers for the guns and eliminating the need to hitch or unhitch the gun from the horse team. This enabled a battery to fire on the move, a significant advantage over its horse-drawn counterparts.

To protect railroad batteries against cannon fire, builders mounted thick iron and wooden shields on the flatcars at a 45 degree angle to deflect enemy projectiles. Batteries fired through the shields and then recoiled along the length of the cars, arrested by ropes. The crews then reloaded the weapons and pushed them back into battery position. The ropes took most of the recoil.

Not all railroad batteries had armor protection. Some relied on mobility covered firing positions and firing during periods of low visibility to limit their exposure to enemy artillery. Other railroad batteries relied on their superior range to batter opposing forces from afar. With such capabilities, railroad artillery was appropriate for siege and

Colonel Charles Dahnmon Whitt

harassment operations as well as head on encounters between armies.

As an army advanced, it often had to rebuild railroads that the fleeing enemy had destroyed. Construction trains, forerunners of modern engineer corps vehicles, thus became indispensable to military operations. These trains required armed protection and infantrymen and cavalrymen often accompanied them.

Also useful in railroad warfare were armed trains, which, as their name implies, carried combat troops and, at times, artillery. Their sequence of cars is noteworthy. The locomotive was placed in the train's center, where it received some protection from the train's cars and its own tender. Generally speaking, flatcars, sometimes loaded with troops and artillery rode at the train's ends to provide the best fields of fire. Passenger cars or boxcars might ride between the flatcars and the locomotive.

Armed trains performed several missions. In some instances they doubled as construction trains. They also patrolled tracks, conducted reconnaissance missions, and escorted supply trains. Individual armed cars also accompanied supply trains, usually coupled to the front of a locomotive. On one occasion, armed Federals in disguise stole a Confederate train and wreaked havoc on the line. Meanwhile, another Federal armed train, only recently commandeered from the Confederates, carried a conventional force through Confederate territory to rendezvous with the renegade train.

Some armed trains carried sandbags or another form of shielding for the troops on board, but this was not always the case. In the first few months of the Civil War, troops disdained cover, since they were accustomed to tactics

Confederate American

best suited for the smoothbore musket. They considered hiding behind cover during combat to be less than manly.

As the war progressed and the killing power of rifled muskets became all too evident, soldiers' attitudes changed toward using cover in combat. Naval events at Hampton Roads, Va., which included a duel between the ironclad vessels *Monitor* and *Merrimack,* convincingly illustrated the efficiency of iron plating in stopping projectiles. Shortly thereafter, *"Monitor fever"* swept the nation as ironclad enthusiasts lobbied for the construction of a huge ironclad fleet. Army officers also caught this fever, and ironclad railroad cars soon appeared across the nation. Fittingly, troops called them railroad monitors, to honor the Federal vessel that inspired the fever.

The first railroad monitors resembled iron boxcars. Light artillery pieces were fired from hatches cut in the hull. Small arms openings cut like small crosses in the sides allowed infantrymen to supplement the fire of the main guns. The car's armor was only thick enough to withstand musket fire; however, commanders generally relegated the boxcar shaped monitors to areas known to be infested with partisans.

Railroad monitors carried several infantrymen. However, firing artillery and muskets from within the cramped confines of a railroad car must have been confusing and dangerous. Ultimately, monitors carried riflemen with repeating rifles inside the car, which had an artillery piece mounted on the top of the car that commanded all sides of the train. This arrangement separated the infantry from the artillery while substantially increasing fire power.

Colonel Charles Dahnmon Whitt

Another means of separating the infantry from the artillery was the rifle car. Rifle cars resembled ordinary boxcars, but their shielding was placed inside the cars. Musket openings on all sides offered their crews wide fields of fire for small arms. Like the artillery railroad monitors, rifle cars could guard key railroad features, protect repairmen, supervise railroad guards and escort supply trains. Just as rifle monitors were the infants of modern tanks, rifle cars were early versions of infantry fighting vehicles.

Along with rifle-cars came a new type of railroad monitor that used thick, sloped iron plates that could deflect light artillery projectiles. This was an important capability when Union horse artillery lurked nearby. These new railroad monitors resembled elongated pyramids and were the same shape as casemated ironclad vessels (turrets were not used with the light artillery on railroad monitors, though armored railroad cars in subsequent conflicts did use turrets). With their thick armor and cannons, these railroad monitors were similar to modern tanks. The Union led in this development because of their resources.

Rifle cars and monitors coupled to a locomotive formed an ironclad train. A simple ironclad train consisted of a locomotive and a railroad monitor. Typically, however, an ironclad train employed a number of cars in a specific sequence as had the armed trains. A railroad monitor rode at each end of the train. Coupled to these were rifle cars, with the locomotive and tender positioned in the middle. This placement distributed firepower evenly, provided mutually supporting small arms and artillery fire, and afforded the locomotive some protection. Not all ironclad trains had the same number of cars, but this placement order became the ideal for armored trains subsequently used by many nations. Indeed, modern armored forces today use a similar combined arms

Confederate American

approach of mutually supporting firepower, although the vehicles operate independently rather than being coupled together in units.

While armor might protect rolling stock from projectiles, explosive devices planted in the roadbed posed serious threats to trains of all types. These torpedoes (known today as mines) included simple artillery shells with percussion fuses as well as specially constructed pressure-detonated devices filled with gunpowder. When buried in the roadbed under a crosstie, torpedoes could be detonated by a passing train. Some torpedoes, especially those using artillery shells, lifted locomotives completely from the tracks and shattered freight cars.

Because of the many hazards that might be present on the tracks, some Federal locomotives pushed loaded flatcars over the rails to inspect the tracks or to detonate torpedoes before the valuable locomotive passed over them. These flatcars offered some protection from mines and from being rammed!

Another method of preventing attacks on Federal trains was to put hostages with Confederate sympathies on the trains. Some Federal commanders even issued sinful decrees threatening to deport local inhabitants or destroy their farms if depredations occurred on local railroads. (Hiding behind women and children.)

Belligerents also used other vehicles on the railroads. Handcars though small were used to inspect rails, transport important personnel and evacuate the wounded. They also helped troops escape superior forces and reconnoiter in better tactical situations. In this role they

Colonel Charles Dahnmon Whitt

were far stealthier than locomotives, although they lacked a locomotive's speed and protective cab. Some handcars were large enough to transport several men, including guards, and were a valuable mode of transport if a locomotive was unavailable. In one instance, a large handcar carried a 10-pounder Parrott gun to duel with a much larger Confederate railroad battery.

Since operable locomotives were at a premium during the war, it was not always economical to use them on missions for which a smaller vehicle would suffice. The Federals therefore applied off-the-shelf technology to warfare, using recently developed steam passenger cars (self-propelled railroad coaches) to inspect the tracks and deliver pay to isolated posts. On such missions, the cars carried some interior armor that protected the steam engine as well as the crew, making the steam passenger cars forerunners of self-propelled armored railroad cars. These heavily armed railroad cars proved good substitutes for armored trains, since several cars were not dependent on a single locomotive for mobility.

Civil War railroad operations were characterized by the widespread use of locomotives and rolling stock to support armies tactically as well as logistically. Americans set precedents for a variety of modern armored fighting vehicles, including armored railroad cars, armored trains, railroad batteries and other railroad weapons. Moreover, tanks, armored personnel carriers, engineer vehicles and self-propelled artillery can also claim American railroad weapons as their conceptual ancestors.

Source: Alan R. Koening

Confederate American

Lee's Men Marching through Fredricksburg, Va.

September 10, 1862

Colonel Charles Dahnmon Whitt

Railroad System in 1861

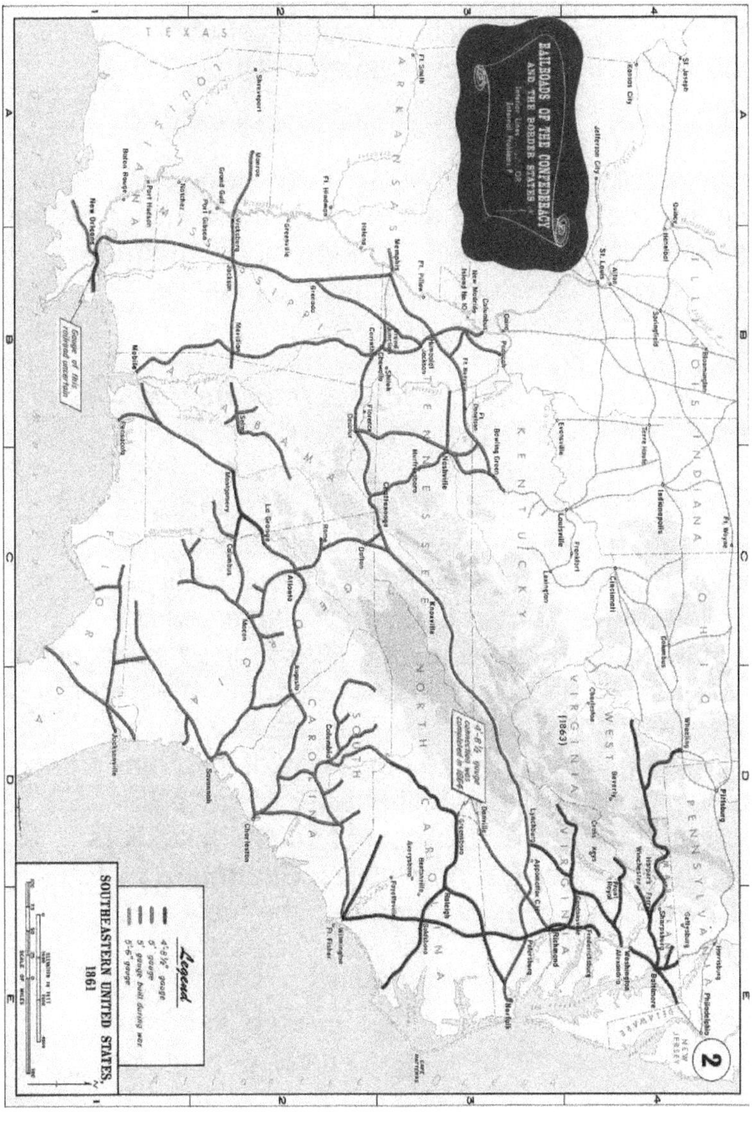

Confederate American

Chapter 7
AWOL

Desertion and AWOL can be different. Desertion means leaving your duty with the intention of never coming back. AWOL (Absent without official leave,) can refer to desertion or temporary absence.

Desertion is not measured by time away from your station, but by leaving or remaining absent from their unit, or place of duty where it looks like the soldier may not return. If that intent is determined to be to avoid danger or obligation it would be desertion.

People who return within 30 days or indicate that they are coming back will be determined AWOL.

Desertion was a major factor for the Confederacy in the last two years of the war. According to Weitz (2000), Confederate soldiers fought to defend their families, not a nation. He argues that a headstrong *"planter class"* brought Georgia into the war with *"little support from non-slaveholders,"* and the ambivalence of non-slaveholders toward secession, he maintains, was the key to understanding desertion. The privations of the home front and camp life, combined with the terror of battle, undermined the weak attachment of southern soldiers to the Confederacy. For Georgia troops, Sherman's march through their home counties triggered the most desertions.

Adoption of a local identity caused soldiers to desert as well. When soldiers implemented a local identity, they

Colonel Charles Dahnmon Whitt

neglected to think of themselves as Southerners fighting a Southern cause. When they replaced their Southern identity with their previous local identity, they lost their motive to fight and therefore, deserted the army.

One example of desertion in the Civil War was Confederate soldier Arthur Muntz, who was killed by his fellow soldiers after deserting at The First Battle of Bull Run. In many cases, in the early years of the war, the Confederate Home Guard dealt with deserters. For a time the Confederate government offered a bounty to be paid for the capture and return of deserters. However, as the war progressively got worse for the south, often Home Guard units would deal with desertion as they saw fit, whether that be by execution or imprisonment. The lynching of Bill Sketoe, a Methodist minister from Newton, Alabama who had allegedly deserted the Southern army in late 1864, is a case in point.

In Arkansas, many units deserted completely when rumors spread that local Indians had raided towns and scalped citizens with the soldiers feeling their place was at home rather than fighting in the war. There were also instances across the southern states where whole units deserted together, and living in the mountains at times fighting against Union Army regulars if forced to do so, but also raiding civilian farms to obtain food or supplies. The fictional story of a wounded Confederate deserter is told in the novel *Cold Mountain*, who at the end of the Civil War walks for months to return home to the love of his life after receiving her letters pleading for him to come home. Many Confederate units had signed on, initially, for a one year service and felt completely justified in walking away when they'd reached their breaking point. By the war's end, it was estimated that the Confederacy had lost 103,400 soldiers to desertion.

Confederate American

The Union Army also faced large scale desertions. Confederate forces lost fewer to desertion than did the northern forces. This has been partly attributed to the Confederate Soldiers fighting a defensive war, on their own ground, rather than an offensive war of invasion which gave the southern soldiers a sense that they were defending their homeland which is always an advantage in any war. In addition, up until late 1863 the South had many victories (in fact more than the North), and many northern soldiers felt the war was a lost cause. For example, New York alone suffered 44,913 desertions by the war's end, with Pennsylvania having 24,050 and Ohio having 18,354, not to mention the desertions faced by the other northern states.

Source: Wikipedia, the free encyclopedia

If Confederates were serving close to home in planting time or harvest or if the family had a large problem or were in danger; often the soldiers would go home and help the family. That is one reason the army wanted to have their soldiers to have some miles between them and home. Often the Army would over look a case where a man went home to plant a field or do some harvesting for the family, but they really frowned on it.

My great Grandfather David Crockett Whitt cut his foot while serving with the Twenty-ninth Virginia; he went home and stayed all winter. His muster reports mentioned he went home with a cut foot, later they even said he cut his foot off. I think his friends were trying to cover for him. Crockett did come back and was captured on the 6th of April 1865.

Colonel Charles Dahnmon Whitt

Chapter 8
Trade Between Yank and Reb

Fraternizing at the Ford
The Rappahannock River During the Civil War

The Yanks and Rebs traded tobacco for coffee by using little boats. This was done between battles.

Confederate American

The Rappahannock River served as a barrier separating the Union and Confederate Armies during the winter of 1862-63. Places where the water level, the river bottom, and the steepness of the banks were favorable for crossings were known as "fords." At Banks' Ford, Alabama troops under Col. Hilary Herbert guarded the Confederate side of the river. Although fraternizing with the enemy was against orders, the opposing soldiers often arranged informal truces.

Warning the Troops
Detachments of soldiers called "pickets" guarded places along the river that were of military value. Their mission was to give warning if an opposing force should advance. The Union pickets in the foreground of this image were directly across the river from this point. Rebs and Yanks enjoying a little friendly poker!

Source Brian Cherry
Anybody who knows about the America Civil War knows that this was one of the most brutal conflicts in human history. To this day the battle of Antietam, one that pitted General Robert E. Lee against the Union's George B. McClellan, still holds the record for the most American military deaths in one day. This includes the United States involvement in the trench warfare of World War I, and the modern mechanized style of fighting of World War II. This along with a number of other vicious battles that often became hand to hand affairs where guys were driving bayonets into the torsos of their fellow man would indicate a deep hatred for the enemy. The surprising thing is this was not the case.

Colonel Charles Dahnmon Whitt

Rebs and Yanks enjoy some poker between battles.

Confederate American

The American Civil War is often credited with the fraternization and making poker into the game we know today. What a lot of people don't know is that the first, informal World Series of Poker may have been played between the enemy soldiers.

The soldiers involved in this war had far more in common than they did reasons to dislike each other. Even the slave issue was generally off the table when it came to the fraternization between Union and Confederate soldiers. The common fighting man didn't have the income to afford a slave, so the issue did not affect them one way or the other. Despite attempts by officers to crackdown on fraternization, casual meetings between northern and southern soldiers were commonplace. While trading goods was one of the major reasons for the meetings (southern boys trading tobacco for coffee with their northern counterparts, etc), poker was a popular way for these guys to spend their time during these unofficial truces.

In the winter of 1862-3 the opposing forces were on either side of Virginia's Rappahannock River. Almost nightly soldiers would meet on a nearby island to trade stories and play some serious poker. Beating your opponent with a pair of Kings seemed much more desirable then trying to shoot him. The game of poker was something common to all of them that transcended politics, propaganda, and war.

Colonel Charles Dahnmon Whitt

General John Brown Gordon

The American Civil War dealt tragedy like no other event in United States history. Despite ubiquitous death and disfiguring wounds, the four years of the Late Unpleasantness cast light on examples of the resilient human spirit.

In early 1865, as Confederate General John Brown Gordon readied his men for an assault on the Union lines at Petersburg, he encountered several now anonymous private soldiers whose enduring spirit would brand lasting

Confederate American

impressions on their commander. Because the opposing lines of the time sat only a few yards apart, secrecy and quiet were crucial elements to the southerner's success. However, while clearing some potential obstructions to their pending assault, a vigilant union soldier shouted over a warning that, if his southern counterpart did not explain the source of this new noise, he would fire. The General would later continue in his memoirs:

"The pickets of the two armies were so close together at this point that there was an understanding between them, either expressed or implied, that they would not shoot each other down except when necessary. The call of this Union picket filled me with apprehension. I expected him to fire and start the entire picket line to firing, thus giving the alarm to the fort, the capture of which depended largely upon the secrecy of my movement. The quick wit of the private soldier at my side came to my relief. In an instant he replied: *"Never mind Yank, lie down and go to sleep. We are just gathering a little corn. You know rations are mighty short over here."*

There was a narrow strip of corn which the bullets had not shot away still standing between the lines. The Union picket promptly answered: "All right, Johnny; go ahead and get your corn. I'll not shoot at you while you are drawing your rations."

Such soldierly courtesy was constantly illustrated between these generous foes, which stood so close to one another in the hostile lines. The Rev. J. William Jones, D.D., now chaplain-general of the United Confederate Veterans, when standing near this same point had his hat carried away by a gust of wind, and it fell near the Union lines.

Colonel Charles Dahnmon Whitt

The loss of a hat meant the loss to the chaplain of nearly a month's pay. He turned away sorrowfully, not knowing how he could get another. A heroic young private, George Haner of Virginia, said to him: *"Chaplain, I will get your hat."* Taking a pole in his hand, he crawled along the ditch which led to our picket-line, and began to drag the hat in with his pole. At this moment a Yankee bullet went through the sleeve of his jacket. He at once shouted to the Union picket: *"Hello Yank quit your foolishness. I am doing no harm. I am just trying to get the chaplain's hat."* Immediately the reply came: *"All right, Johnny; I'll not shoot at you any more. You'd better hurry up and get it before the next relief comes."*

My troops stood in close column, ready for the hazardous rush upon Fort Stedman. While the fraternal dialogue in reference to drawing private at my side the last of the obstructions in my front were removed and I ordered the private to fire the signal for the assault. He pointed his rifle upward with his finger on the trigger but hesitated. His conscience seemed to get hold of him. He was going into the fearful charge, and he evidently did not feel disposed to go into eternity with the lie on his lips, although it might be a permissible war lie, by which he had thrown the Union picket off his guard. He evidently felt that it was hardly fair to take advantage of the generosity and soldierly sympathy of his foe, who had so magnanimously assured him that he would not be shot while drawing his rations from the little field of corn. His hesitation surprised me and I again ordered: "Fire your gun, sir." He at once called to his kindhearted foe and said:

"Hello, Yank! Wake up we are going to shell the woods. Look out we are coming." And with this effort to satisfy his conscience and even up accounts with the Yankee picket, he fired the shot and rushed forward in the darkness."

Confederate American

Chapter 9

Lee's Measurables, POW

This is an Insert out of the Book, "Legacy, The Days Of David Crockett Whitt,"

"Crockett," is the name of my Great Grandfather that served in the Twenty-ninth, Virginia Infantry This account was just after the battle of Saylor's Creek. Crockett and his band of brothers escaped the Yankees and got left behind by the Confederate Army. They had enjoyed a meal of pork with some run away slaves. For more information read the book, "Legacy, The Days of David Crockett Whitt."

They (Crockett and his band of brothers) moved about a mile west on the road to Farmville and found another thicket to hide in. Having a meal in their belly they all fell into deep sleep. This was the morning of April 7th, 1865. After hiding out most of the day and traveling the thickets beside the road they were close to Farmville. Crockett thanked God for his loving kindness and the meal of pork they had received.

They traveled the night of the 7th and had to jump and hide again. This time a band of lost Confederates were captured less than one hundred yards from Crockett and the five. Yankee Cavalry swooped out of nowhere on the unsuspecting gray backs and marched them toward

Colonel Charles Dahnmon Whitt

Farmville.

Crockett and the five talked about their situation and wondered about the wisdom of heading to Farmville. They reasoned that they should skirt around the town and try to catch up with the main body at a later date. They were close enough to Farmville to hear many Yankee's talking and realized they should avoid the town.

The morning of April 8th was coming with the rising sun. It was time to find a suitable hiding place. They were fortunate to find another thicket large enough to hide all of them. Crockett and his circle of friends quietly ate their last morsel of pig bacon and lay down to sleep. They did not sleep too much this day as the Yanks kept the road hot as they were rounding up more poor Rebels. Also more and more army was on the chase to catch up with General Lee.

Crockett and the circle of friends reasoned together as to what course of action they should take. Some wanted to follow the main body of Lee's Army, while others thought they should just strike out to the south and get away from this place.

"If we stay around here we will just be captured and taken to one of those awful prisons," said one of the six.

Crockett was one of the first to say out loud what they all were thinking.

"I am true to Virginia, but I am afraid we have a lost cause and must get away from the Yanks before we are carried off," Crockett said.

"I agree with Crockett, we should strike out for home, if we

Confederate American

run into our army we can join back up," said Isaac Puckett.

They all agreed and tried to get some rest before the night came again. Just in the twilight, on the evening of April the 8th 1865 the six Confederates eased out on the road and crossed over to the other side. They had gone less than a mile when two groups of mounted men merged on them from both the east and the west. It was too late to run. The Yankee's captured Crockett and the other five. They were held with shotguns, and .44 caliber revolvers.

A mouthy Yankee sergeant did the talking.
"Well hello Johnny Reb, just where are you off to?" he asked.

Isaac spoke up and said, "We are heading home Sergeant, we have had enough of this war," trying to convince the captors to let them go.

"Well not today, you ain't going nowhere," answered the sergeant.

They were marched about a mile into Farmville and each was questioned for about an hour each. Finally an officer told them to lock up the six in a big barn along with some more of the captured Southerners. Water, a piece of pork and bread was brought out and given to each man. Crockett took time to thank God for the food and for sparing the lives of his friends.

When Crockett was being questioned, he answered truly and frankly. The young Union Officer was not the overbearing man Crockett expected. He made Crockett

Colonel Charles Dahnmon Whitt

feel at ease as he questioned him. Crockett sat and the young man paced.

"Private what is your name?" he asked.

"David Crockett Whitt, sir," Crockett answered.
   "Well private, how did you get a name like that?" he asked.

"Well sir, I was born in 1836 the year of the Alamo, David Crockett was famous, so my Maw named me after him," Crockett answered.

"Well David how many *"Darkies"* do you have on your place?" he continued.

"None sir, I don't own no slaves," Crockett answered.

None, well how come you are fighting against the United States?" asked the young officer.

"Cause you all are down here attacking our country," Crockett answered.

"Well David what makes you think you can secede from the union?" he asked.

"Well not to be testy sir, if you would go back in history to March 4th 1789 the Union was formed. Each State had to decide if they wanted to join or not. There was nothing written down about not letting a state out and that was on purpose you see," said Crockett.

"When New York, Rhode Island, and Virginia ratified the Constitution they specifically stated that they have the right to go back and govern themselves. The right of

Confederate American

secession was understood and agreed to even George Washington who presided over the Constitutional Convention was a delegate from Virginia. You see sir the Constitution was an experiment and the folks here in Virginia wanted their Independence." continued Crockett.

"Are you saying that if we had not crossed over into Virginia there would be no war?" asked the officer.

"That is purty much right, I reckon," replied Crockett.

"Well how come you fellers invaded Gettysburg?" the officer asked.

"Well I reckon after almost three years of fighting here, General Lee decided to give the North some of the same," Crockett answered.

"David, do you know where Bob Lee is heading for?" asked the officer.

"West I reckon, that is about all I know not to be smart, we privates are not privy to all the information," Crockett answered.

"Did you know that General Lee and General Grant are talking surrender terms?" he asked.

"No sir, all I know is that you alls cavalry cut us all apart back at Sayler's Creek and we have been trying to get out of this place," Crockett answered.

"Me and my friends had decided to strike out for home when you fellers caught us," continued Crockett.

Colonel Charles Dahnmon Whitt

"You mean desert, David?" the officer asked.

"Well in a way that would be right, but the way we looked at it is the army deserted us and we just wanted to get away from you fellers," Crockett answered.

"You boys sure look poor and ragged, are you ready to get something to eat Private?" the young officer asked.

"I reckon I could eat something sir'" Crockett replied.

"Well you go with the private and he will see you fellers get some food," ordered the officer.

"Thanks sir, could you tell me sir, what are you going to do with me and my five friends?" Crockett asked.

"You will be transported tomorrow to Point Lookout Prison, then I reckon after the war you can go back home. Thank you David for talking with me and I hope we will all be countrymen sometime down the road," the young officer said.

Crockett was not pleased to hear Point Lookout; all he ever heard of that place was bad. Folks called the unlucky people that ended up there, "Lee's Miserables"

Well I guess I better try to explain one thing at this time. All of my research stated that David Crockett Whitt was captured on April 6th 1865 near Farmville Virginia. I went with April the 8th 1865, because Crockett personally stated on his war disability application to Virginia on May 15th 1906, which he was captured near Farmville, Virginia the evening before Lee surrendered. He plainly wrote April 8th

Confederate American

1865. Well I guess some folks may disagree with me, but if he was at Cold Harbor, Drewry's Bluff, and many other encounters, including shivering in the trenches of Bermuda Hundred line and about three months in the hell of Point Lookout, an old man should know when he was captured. Crockett was sixty nine when he applied for disability from Virginia. By the way the, Northern Troops got their Veteran's Benefits shortly after the war from the United States. I guess it mattered which side you were on.

Next day General Lee and General Grant would meet at the McLean's House in Appomattox, Virginia. This place was picked because it lay between the two Generals. The Northern Army had surrounded the Confederates on three sides and left Lee with little choice. The Confederates lost time at Sayler's Creek and more time when Lee sent out men to forage for food around the country side.

General Lee sent out flags of truce and asked Grant to meet with him and talk on the matter of conditions he previously offered. Grant was traveling from Farmville toward Appomattox Court House to set up a new headquarters. Grant looked improperly dressed for such an occasion, but the traveling on muddy roads and fording the Appomattox River left him mud spattered and in an unmilitary look. He was most anxious to meet with General Lee, and maybe end this awful war.

General Robert E. Lee donned his new gray uniform on the evening of April 8th. I don't know why he dug it out and put it on that evening unless he was pretty sure of meeting Grant. The next day he rode about two miles to meet at the McLean House. After negotiating the conditions of surrender, Lee surrendered the Army of

Colonel Charles Dahnmon Whitt

Northern Virginia, not the whole Army. Lee surrendered 28,231 men.

After the fighting at Sayler's Creek, General William Nelson Pendleton was nominated by other high ranking officers to speak to General Lee about surrender. Pendleton and Lee sat under a pine tree and talked about the subject on the morning of April 7th 1865. When the talk was over Lee thanked him for his and the other officers input. General Lee said, "I trust it has not come to that. We certainly have too many brave men to think of laying down our arms, indeed, we must all determine to die at our post."

On the evening of April 7th, General Lee received a dispatch from General Grant.

General R. E. Lee.
  Commanding C. S. Army:
  General: The result of the last week must convince you of the hopelessness of further resistance on the part of the Army of Northern Virginia in this struggle. I feel that it is so and regard it as my duty to shift from myself the responsibility of any further effusion of blood, by asking of you to surrender of that portion of the C. S. Army known as the Army of Northern Virginia.
  Very respectfully, your obedient servant,
  U. S. Grant
  Lieutenant-General
  Commanding Armies of the United States

General Lee read the dispatch carefully and turned to General Longstreet his trusted subordinate and let him read the dispatch.

"Not yet," answered General Longstreet.

Confederate American

With the meeting this morning with General Pendleton, now the dispatch from Grant, it was weighting heavily on General Lee's mind. Lee chewed on it for two more days before coming to a decision.

After the surrender General Lee issued General Order, No. 9. April 10, 1865.

General Lee told his Adjutant-General Lieutenant Colonel Charles Marshall to compose a document. He expressed to Marshall his feelings toward the men of the Army of Northern Virginia.

After Marshall finished the rough draft he gave it to General Lee to read. Lee made minor changes and completely omitted one paragraph that Lee thought would insight bitterness between the Union and the defeated Confederates. Copies were made in ink and given to the Corps Commanders to read to their men.

After four years of arduous service, marked by unsurpassed courage and fortitude, the Army of Northern Virginia has been compelled to yield to overwhelming numbers and resources.

I need not tell the brave survivors of so many hard fought battles, who have remained steadfast to the last, that I have consented to this result from no distrust of them.

But feeling that valor and devotion could accomplish nothing that would compensate for the loss that must have attended the continuance of the contest, I determined to avoid the useless sacrifice of those past services have endeared them to their countrymen.

By the terms of the agreement officers and men can return to their homes and remain until exchanged. You will

Colonel Charles Dahnmon Whitt

take with you the satisfaction that proceeds from the consciousness of duty faithfully performed, and I earnestly pray that a Merciful God will extend to you His blessing and protection.

With an increasing admiration of your constancy and devotion to your country and a grateful remembrance of your kind and generous consideration for myself, I bid you all an affectionate farewell. R. E. Lee General

Crockett along with his five friends and many more captured men began to trudge toward Point Lookout on the morning of April 9th 1865. They were a poor defeated lot. As they marched along in the early afternoon the Union guards and officers began to celebrate and cheer. Before any of the prisoners could even ask, the Yankee's started shouting, "Lee has surrendered."

Crockett's heart leaped, could this be true and does this mean they will let us go home? It wasn't long before he got the answer, as the overbearing guards goaded them on. One of the prisoners asks why they couldn't turn them loose, and a guard went over and slapped him on top of the head with rein of his horse.

"You Damn Rebels have killed my friends and even my brother, now by God you are going to pay," said the belligerent Yankee.

"Besides that, you stupid Confederates would go and join up with Johnston and we would have to fight you again," continued the guard.

An officer rode up and pulled the guard to the side and spoke to him in a low tone. Crockett heard the guard say, "Yes I understand, Sir."

Confederate American

Crockett figured that the men had orders not to physically abuse them unless provoked. Crockett hoped that the officers would stay close.

Some of the guards kept saying over and over, "Lee has surrendered and we have a grand General, Grant is the best in the land."

The defeated Rebels held their tongues, as they marched along. They all felt like they would be turned loose before long since General Lee surrendered. Crockett and his five friends stuck together like glue and all were thankful to be alive. Crockett thanked God for his protection and prayed for freedom to go home to his little family.

The prisoners heard that all the Confederate Soldiers that were at Appomattox were given food and some were able to take a mule or horse and head for home. Why are we still marching on to Point Lookout? It became evident that the soldiers had a vendetta against the captured Southerner's. Crockett would just have to bide his time and stay out of trouble with these angry Yanks. Crockett was now one of, "*Lee's Miserables*," since he was on his way to Point Lookout Prison Pen.

I had mentioned earlier that the 29th Infantry was the largest in Corse's Brigade. On April 9th 1865, Lee surrendered only 30 men of the Twenty-ninth. The rest were either killed, captured, hospitalized, or wandering the countryside. The ranking officer of the now small 29th Infantry was First Lieutenant John Alexander Coulson of Company C and this made him the commanding officer at the time of surrender.

Colonel Charles Dahnmon Whitt

Crockett arrived across the bay from Point Lookout at City Point on April 13th 1865 along with hundreds of Confederate Prisoners of war. Steamers were waiting to transport the defeated southern men. The march from Farmville had not been too hard, and all the men had received crackers and meat. The Yankee soldiers were not friendly to the troop of gray clad men of the Army of Northern Virginia.

Most every Yankee harbored resentment for what they called the Rebels. Any chance they had they abused the poor undernourished and worn "Sons of the South."

Crockett and his friends said little as they journeyed overland, but stayed close to each other. Now they saw the steamers waiting to take them across the Potomac River, the upper part of the bay to Point Lookout.

The six friends from southwest Virginia stuck together like glue as the Yankee's crowded the southerners on the steamers. They put so many men on each boat it was standing room only. The Captain complained to the Federal officer that the boat was at risk of going down in the bigger than usual waves caused by the spring winds.

"Hell, that wouldn't be no big loss, cept for the boat and one fussy captain," said the officer.

"That ain't one bit funny," replied the captain.

"Go on and take this worthless load cross the bay and get back we got to get it done," continued the officer.

The boat captain shook his head from side to side as he hollered, "cast off."

Confederate American

Crockett and his friends were on the front of the boat. They looked in the direction the boat was traveling and saw the hazy form of land and some buildings. They all talked quietly together about their fate and the need to stay together. A guard saw them talking and hollered at them.

"Hey you stupid Rebels close them traps," said the young guard with both hands on his musket.

Crockett and Isaac Puckett both nodded their heads at the guard and quit talking.

As the boat pulled into the dock at Point Lookout, they were greeted by two lines of insolent Negro Yankee guards.

"Yaw com on in, welcome to Point Lookout," said one of the black soldiers.

"The worm has turned, now your asses belong to us," another one hollered.

"How you boys like being the slaves?" another one asked.

A white Union Major, the Provost Marshall, A.G. Brady rode up on his horse, and the Negro guards became quiet. He addressed the boat load of ragged Confederate's.

"I am Major Brady, the Provost Marshall here at this institution. I am the law here, you will obey every order you receive or die. Try to escape and you will die. Behave and someday you will go home. Welcome to the Federal

Colonel Charles Dahnmon Whitt

camp, Point Lookout," said Major Brady as he wheeled his steed around and rode off.

The following statement was given by Charles T. Loehr, October 11, 1890. He was one of the captured Confederates housed in Point Lookout captured during the battle of Five Forks, Virginia.

"He wrote in his little New Testament on June 3rd 1865, ("If it were not for hope, how could we live in a place like this? Point Lookout, June 3rd, 1865.")

"In turning back to those dark days of our country's history I do so simply to present these facts and incidents in which I was a participant. I want to show how the Confederate soldier suffered even after General Lee had bid his farewell to his army at Appomattox. The "surrender at Appomattox," so often quoted by our Southern orators to denote "the soldier who has done his duty," is but partly true.

General Lee surrendered about 26,000 men, of whom only 7,892 were armed. A greater part of them were men that were on detail duty, or held some position which kept them safely in the rear. It is a fact that few, very few, indeed, of General Ewell's and Pickett's men escaped from those that stood in battle line doing their duty on the evening of April 6, 1865.

At the bloody ridge of Sailor's Creek the men that were left there had a forlorn hope of fighting, with few exceptions, were captured or killed and I assert without fear of contradiction that there were more fighting men at the close of the war in Point Lookout Prison alone, not to mention Fort Delaware, Hart's Island, Johnson's Island, Newport's news, and other questionable places of amusement, than there were in Lee's whole army at the

Confederate American

surrender, I make the remarks necessary in justice to the Confederate soldiers who suffered and starved in the fearful prison-pens of the North, but did not "Surrender at Appomattox."

At City Point several transport steamers were lying and we were ordered on board of them each boat being packed with human freight to its full capacity.

Some of the boats landed their unwilling passengers at Newport's News, while most of them and the one I was on, reached Point Lookout on the morning of the 5th. (Crockett arrived on the 14th.) Landing at the wharf, we were formed in open line for inspection; that is, we had to empty our pockets and lay our baggage on the ground before us, while the Federal sergeants amused themselves by kicking overcoats, blankets, oilcloths, canteens, and everything that had a U.S. on it, into the bay. This left us in a sad condition, for there was little in our possession that had not been the property of the United States, at one time or another, and became ours by the many victories and captures we had helped to gain.

After putting us in light marching order we were marched into the prison-pen, or *"bull-pen,"* as it was called. The prison consisted of a space of about twenty acres surrounded by a high board fence on the outside of which was the top a platform for the guard to walk upon. The guards consisted of Negroes of the worst sort. Inside the grounds, about fifteen feet of the fence, was a ditch called the *"dead line."* The sentry fired upon anyone who crossed it.

The camp was laid in regular rows of small tents, each

Colonel Charles Dahnmon Whitt

double row being a division, of which there were ten. These were again sub-divided into ten companies of about two hundred men each. Through these streets or rows there ran small ditches; but the land being very shallow, the drainage was very imperfect. Point Lookout being a tongue of land where the Potomac and Chesapeake Bay, barely five feet at it's highest point; and herein was the worst feature of the prison. There was no good drinking water to be had; the water was impregnated with copperas, and tasted quiet brackish. To this source was a great deal of the fearful mortality that occurred there traceable.

When we came there the prison was already full, and the small tents were totally insufficient to accommodate us. Many were without shelter of any kind, and exposed to the bad weather which prevailed for the greater part of our stay. We had but few blankets, and most had to lie on the bare ground; so when it rained our situation became truly deplorable. Our rations were just such as kept us perpetually on the point of starvation, causing a painful feeling of hunger to us helpless-starved prisoners. Four small crackers, or a small loaf of bread per day, and a cup full of dish-water, called pea-soup, horrible to taste, and a small piece of rancid salt meat, was our daily fare. So hungry were the men that they would eat almost anything they could pick up outside from the sewers; potato peelings, cabbage stalks, or most any refuse that hardly the cattle would eat, was greedily devoured. The scurvy, brought on by this wretched diet, was prevalent in its most awful form.

It was not unusual to hear it stated that sixty or sixty-five deaths had occurred in a single day; and it was said that eight thousand six hundred dead Confederates were buried near the prison pen. (14,000 were accounted for by

Confederate American

letters and other sources)

It is wonderful how much a human being can stand. I myself (Charles T. Loehr), who was never sick during the whole war, was taken down with erysipelas. It was a bad case, so said the Federal surgeon said who examined me. "Entirely too late to do anything for him; neck and face swollen black and green." Those who did the packing up, that is placing the dead bodies in rough boxes, seeing me, one of them said, "There goes a fellow we will have to box up tomorrow." I was removed to the hospital pen, and with two of my company Alexander Moss and John Harris, both of whom I saw stretched out in the dead house on the following day. The hospital could only accommodate about twelve hundred sick, and there were no less than six thousand sick and dying men within the main building and tents surrounding it. Being assigned to a tent there was room for about sixteen, but which had no less than forty in it, I was placed on the damp ground, only one thin blanket being given me. The two nights I spent there were simply horrible. The praying, crying and the fearful struggles of the dying during the dark night, lit up by a single small lantern, were awful. The first night about five or six died, and the next morning found me lying next to two dead comrades. The second night was a repetition of the first; and that day, though just in the same condition, I asked the Federal surgeon to return to camp, which was granted, thinking I might just as well die there as anywhere else. But I got better, how I cannot explain; perhaps it was my determination not to die there in spite of them that kept me alive.

Great as the sufferings of the men were from want of sufficient food and medicines, they were much increased

Colonel Charles Dahnmon Whitt

from want of clothing. Some were nearly naked, only one ragged shirt to wear, and this covered with vermin. On an occasion of Major A. J. Brady's (Provost Marshall) visit to the camp, which happened on an unusually bright day, the men were seated in the ditch in front of their tents, busy hunting for the tormentors, having their only garment off, using it for the field to hunt in. (Lice and Insects were the prey), Brady smilingly remarked to some who through modesty attempted to hide, "Don't stop, I like to see you busy."

Talking of Major Brady, no one can say that he was not always polite, and he appeared to be friendly towards the prisoners, (other accounts paint a different picture of him) yet it is said that he made more than $1,000,000 dollars outside his pay, from his position. Having charge of all the sultler establishments, and all the money, boxes, letters and presents passing through or in his hands, his position must have made him a rich man.

Next our guards: As already stated, they were Negroes who took particular delight in showing their former masters that "The bottom of rail was the top." On one occasion one of the North Carolina men, who have a habit, which is shared by our Virginia Country cousins, in whittling every wooden object they come across, was enjoying this sport on the prison gate, when one of the colored soldiers shot him down, nearly blowing his head off. This created some little excitement, but what the result was I never learned. During the day we had access to the sink built on piles in the bay, but at night the gates were closed, and boxes were placed in the lower part of the camp, to which the men were allowed to go at all hours of the night. There were hundreds of sick in camp, cases of violent diarrhea, reducing the men to skeletons.

Confederate American

As these men were compelled to frequent these boxes, the Negroes would often compel them at the point of the bayonet to march around in double quick time, to carry them on their backs, to kneel and pray for Abe Lincoln, and forced them to submit to a variety of their brutal jokes, some of which decency would not permit me to mention.

The white sergeants in charge were hardly of a better class than their colored brother. They belonged to that class of mean cowards who dare not face the foe on the battle field, whose bravery consisted in insulting and maltreating a defenseless prisoner. Often I have seen them kick a poor, sick, broken-down prisoner, because he was physically unable to take his place in line at roll-call as quickly as the sergeant demanded. Prisoners were sometimes punished by them too horribly to relate. Men were tied, hand and feet, and had to stand on a barrel for hours; others were bound and dipped head foremost in a urine barrel-all this for some trifling offence, such as getting water from a prohibited well, stealing perhaps something eatable, or some other small affair.

But most things, whether good or bad, will come to an end. More than two months had passed since Lee's surrender. The Confederacy was no more, and the Federal Government took courage. About the middle of June it commenced to release those that were still living, but, in consequence of the inhuman treatment they had received, too feeble to fight again. Then we were duly sworn not to fight them again, to support the Constitution and amendments. Also registering our good looks, weight, height, &c., and getting our signatures made as free men again."

Colonel Charles Dahnmon Whitt

The above report by Charles T. Loehr has been proven out by other accounts by prisoners locked away in the damp mire of Point Lookout Prison Pen.

On the 14th of April, 1865 Crockett and his five friends stepped off the boat and fell into lines as directed by Yankee sergeants and the Negro guards. They were instructed to empty their pockets and lay all of their gear on the ground for inspection.

"Johnny Reb, you ain't in the United States Army so anything got U.S. on it, take it off and throw it with the rest of the baggage on the ground," yelled the belligerent sergeant.

Most of the Southern soldiers had mostly U.S. things that had been captured in many big battles. Coats, blankets, canteens, and many other items were cast on the ground. The Negro's made a game of kicking the piles of clothing and supplies into the bay. Crockett along with the rest of the captives stood there in disbelief. Most of the men had only ragged paints and shirts, very few blankets made it through this so called inspection. The men were to bear the elements in thin ragged clothes.

Next the men were marched through the gate of Point Lookout Pen where Crockett saw thousands of countrymen wasting away in this small plot of about twenty acres. There was row after row of small weathered tents. Crockett had heard stories of this place, but nothing compared to the reality he saw.

Crockett and his five friends were marched to a place in the pen and halted. One of the sergeants yelled out, "You six are now in Company D, 7th Division, Point Lookout Prisoner of War Camp, remember it."

Confederate American

The six said nothing, but stood there at attention.

"Can't you Johnny's speak, say yes Sir," when you hear an order.

"Yes Sir," replied all the men in this line.

"This here tent is yours, least when it gets vacated," grunted the sergeant.

"Dismissed," yelled the sergeant.

Crockett and the others looked in the ragged decaying tent and saw two sickly men lying on the bare ground. Crockett stood up and scanned the surroundings. He saw the wall with the black guards looking menacing at the thousands of southern men. They were just itching to shoot into the crowds. Crockett also saw the ditch that ran around the pen about fifteen feet from the stockade; this was the "Dead Line." It was explained by the sergeant earlier that any prisoner crossing it would be shot down.

Some of the healthier prisoners came up and introduced themselves to the new arrivals. After talking some and asking questions Crockett decided to sit down and rest as did the other men. Something dreadful happened; their bodies began to burn and sting. Crockett lifted his shirt and found he was covered with body lice.

"My God, I am being eaten alive," said Burdell Brewster one of the circle of friends.

The men that had been there for some time began to

Colonel Charles Dahnmon Whitt

laugh!

"Ain't really funny, son," said one of the older prisoners.

"But we got to find something to laugh about in this hell hole," he added.

"What do you do about them?" Crockett asked in a serious tone.

"Don't worry they won't eat you up, jest pick um off," replied the older man.

"Hell I got me a fat one I keep under my arm, he's the biggest bastard in the bunch," replied another man.

"What for?" asked Crockett.

"I can produce him for winning a bet, since no bodies got nutt-un, no how, I jest yanks him out for show," he said as he reached under his left arm pit and brought out a whopper of a louse.

The six new arrivals found one thing to laugh about.

Isaac Puckett spoke up, "Hold on to your faith men, nothing last forever, the war is over, surely the Yanks will let us go home any day."

Crockett looked at him and smiled.

"With what we been through in the past few years, we can survive this," Crockett said.

Back in Tazewell County Arminda has learned that General Lee has surrendered and Crockett should be

Confederate American

coming home any day. She cleaned the house, got all the clothes washed, and readied for her beloved husband.

Everyone in Baptist Valley was saddened by the news that General Lee surrendered, but was glad their men would be coming home. A few made their way back home in their ragged clothes. They were for the most part skinny and worn. Crockett and his five friends did not show up!

"My God, where is my husband," declared Arminda.

Rhoda and her family had Arminda and the babies over for supper and held a prayer meeting for Crockett and others that had not made it home. John Bunyan Lowe and Rhoda tried to console Arminda.

"Crockett is not dead, the Yankee's must have him in one of those prisons," said Rhoda.

"The war is bout over, so they will be letting our boys come home," declared John Bunyan Lowe.
Arminda took hope as she did not have a feeling reflecting that Crockett was dead. After talking to the Lord and hearing others lifting up Crockett in prayer and hearing the family's words of encouragement,

Arminda felt sure he would return.

After spending a terrible night at Point Lookout, the morning of April 15th 1865 brought reality to David Crockett Whitt. Yes this is real, not a nightmare, but a nightmare that is here and now. After going through the morning hours, and learning the ways of the prison, all hell broke loose.

Colonel Charles Dahnmon Whitt

Major Brady (Provost Marshall) comes riding his big footed horse up and down the rows or streets of the entire compound. The poor Confederates scattered to keep from being trampled. Brady was shouting, "Lincoln is dead, you damn Rebs will pay for this."

The Black guards went berserk and many of them fired into the compound. Crockett and his five friends hit the ground getting behind any cover available.

Major Brady had learned this morning that last night at the Ford Theater in Washington D.C.; President Abraham Lincoln had been assassinated by John Wilkes Booth. All of the Union soldiers were saddened and wanted revenge. The poor underfed, half-naked Confederate soldiers in the prisons were at their mercy.

Crockett and others discussed this in whispering tones and decided the only course was to stay out of the Yankee's way and stay humble. Each one also prayed for the loving God of heaven to protect them. One of the men had a little book of the Psalms; he opened it to his favorite the 91st. He read it aloud to Crockett and the men that were gathered around him.

After the reading Crockett said, "This Psalm is all about God giving protection to those that love Him."

"Amen!" said Isaac Puckett.

Somehow no one was injured by the horse or the shots that were fired into the pen that day. All day long the Negroes yelled slurs at the prisoners and pronounced vengeance on them. They pointed their muskets and made gestures at the men. The men were quiet and

Confederate American

hardly moved all day long. No rations were given to them this day.

Crockett borrowed a Bible and was led to the 3rd chapter of Ecclesiastes. He read it over and thought it over. He went to his friends to share the message. Crockett told them he wanted them to hear this word of God that proved nothing is permanent and that all things are temporary, even this hell hole they now lived in would end.

Crockett turned to the marked page in the little Bible, and read.

Ecclesiastes 3: 1-8

1. To every thing there is a season, and a time to every purpose under the heaven:

2. A time to be born, and a time to die; a time to plant, and a time to pluck up that which is planted:

3. A time to kill, and a time to heal; a time to break down, and a time to build up;

4. A time to weep, and a time to laugh; a time to mourn, and a time to dance;

5. A time to cast away stones, and a time to gather; a time to embrace, and a time to refrain from embracing;

6. A time to get, and a time to lose; a time to keep, and a time to cast away;

7. A time to rend, and a time to sow; a time to keep silence, and a time to speak;

8. A time to love, and a time to hate; a time of war and a time of peace.

After the reading, the men all had comments, reflecting that if they could just stay alive, a new season would come and they all could go home. All of the men listening took hope and thanked Crockett for reading the word to

Colonel Charles Dahnmon Whitt

them.

It was a good thing Spring was here, but on this slab of beach the pen was located on was surrounded by water. April nights and some days were really chilly because of the constant wind and the men had thin ragged clothes. About one blanket per 16 men was the average. The highest ground of the camp was only about five feet above the water. Little fire wood was available.

Crockett and his five friends had been in the pen for about a week, when one night a strong wind came up. The extra high tide came into the camp, even into the tents, and the men had to get up from their sleep and stand up until the waves subsided. Many of the sick and weak had to be held up as best they could. Many days sixty to sixty five Confederates died, but after this night over 300 died because of exposure.

It took every ounce of hope to survive there with the lack of food, and the lack of the simple necessities of life. The men were so hungry, they would eat most anything. Dead fish washed up and were consumed, or an occasional rat would make the misfortune and wander into the camp. The men found that rat meat was quite good.

In its living conditions and treatment of prisoners, Point Lookout has often been compared to Andersonville, the Confederate prison for Union troops in Georgia. The mortality rate at Point Lookout was greater than that of the Confederate prison at Andersonville. Moreover, the fatalities at Point Lookout were due to unnecessary neglect, while those at Andersonville were due to a real want in the Confederacy as a whole. The United States War Department's official statistics showed that more Southern prisoners died in Northern Camps than did

Confederate American

Northern soldiers die in Southern camps. The death rate in Northern camps was 12%, while the rate in Southern camps was about 9%. The people in the South were starving by the end of the war and couldn't feed their own troops, but the North had no such excuse.

It was on purpose, the treatment prisoners received in Northern prisons to weaken and destroy the enemy of the United States. Both houses of the U.S. Congress passed HR 97 which was designed to slowly eliminate the Southern prisoners. If anything qualifies an outrage surely this does.

Crockett leaned heavily on the Lord and his five earthly friends to get by each day. As bad as the war was this Pen was even worse.

Finally, toward the end of May 1865, some good people brought paper, pens, ink and postage stamps and gave it to the prisoners. Major Brady let the men have them, he figured it would keep them busy and it didn't come out of his funds. He did lay down the law to each prisoner, that nothing could be written derogatory of the Point Lookout Prison. Each letter had to be delivered to the officers unopened. The officers would read through and censor anything they thought should not be in it. They would destroy the whole letter if they thought it made the North look bad. Only one page was allowed to be mailed.

Crockett was thrilled to be able to write home. He composed a one page letter to Arminda telling how he loved her and that he would come home as soon as possible. He also wrote a letter to his father Jonas Whitt in Greenup County, Ky. He asked Jonas to help expedite his

Colonel Charles Dahnmon Whitt

release. Many of the prisoners were not well educated and had bad penmanship so Crockett helped a number of them write a letter home. He remembered how Samuel Truitt made him practice writing each letter over and over in the little school house at Truittville, Kentucky. Crockett felt fortunate and glad to be able to do something for his comrades, his education paid off. Now if these pesky lice would leave him alone, he thought as he scratched at the little tormentors.

Below is a bona-fide letter written by David Crockett Whitt.
Point-Lookout, May 30"65
Dear Father
You will no doubt be surprised to receive a letter from me from this place. I arrived here 14" April was captured on the 8" near Farmville, Va. I have signified my willingness to take the oath of allegiance. I wish you to go to work and try to get me released as soon as possible. I think if you make an effort you will be successful. I belonged to Co "H" 29" Va. Regt. If you can do nothing, get my brother in law Thompson (Alfred) to do what he can. I have 5 comrades in here if you can get them released by vouching for them, I would like to have it done so. Their names are Burdell Brester, J. W. Birchem, D. C. Lewis, Isaac Puckett, and Ias Colston all of my regt. Do what ever you can for me and write.
Your Aff. Son David C. Whitt
   Prisoner of war; Co" D, 7" Div. Point Lookout Maryland

The letter was of excellent penmanship and well written all on one small sheet of paper. Here it was the 30th of May and the Yankee's were still holding them. Lee had surrendered way back on the 9th of April 1865 and they were still living a hell on earth at Point Lookout.

It is likely that Jonas Whitt never saw this letter as he

Confederate American

passed away on July 2nd 1865. I don't know if Jonas had time or if Alfred Thompson took steps to have Crockett released.

Finally in June 1865 the United States started releasing the Confederate Prisoners of war. In the month of April 1865 12,110 men joined the ranks of POW's in Point Lookout. On hand at Point Lookout, on May 31st 1865 were 18,365 men. Released in June were 18,536. Some of the men were released and died not being able to leave the God forsaken place.

Crockett survived the rancid food, the ill-treatment, the exposure to weather, and all the evil Negro guards could deal out. He was finally selected for parole, and released on June 22nd 1865.

The selected prisoners having lived through the season of hate now were coming into the season of "Going home." Things good or bad all come to a conclusion in time. The Confederacy was no more and the Federal Government took courage. It started to release those that were still living, but, in consequence of the inhuman treatment they had received, were too feeble to fight again. Then they were duly sworn not to fight them again, to support the Constitution, and amendments. Charles T. Loehr said, "Registering our good looks, weight, height, and getting our signatures made us free men again. Crockett was listed as fair complexion, brown hair; eyes were gray, height 5 feet 11 ½ inches tall. No weight was listed.

A new season has come to Point Lookout and Crockett was glad! The Federal Government is finally letting the Confederate prisoners out and just in time, another month

Colonel Charles Dahnmon Whitt

or so and many more would die. Crockett with the last name of Whitt, beginning with "W" was let out later than his five friends. His friend Isaac Puckett headed to Russell, County on the 16th of June. Crockett felt lost without his close friends, but all the men were friends because they were all in the same situation.

Finally a Yankee sergeant came and got Crockett on the 21st of June and took him to another holding pen for paroled prisoners. By now the prison looked bare, yet it still housed hundreds. In the new pen they were properly whitewashed to kill the lice. This was an enclosed space adjoining the hospital on the east, where nothing but sand and some rank weeds could be found. Here the released prisoners were stored until a sufficient number were on hand to make up a boat load.

On the 22nd of June 1865 the paroled men were ushered into a big tent where they stood in front of Major Brady. He had them place hands on Bibles, as many as six to a Bible, and say the oath that they had already signed.

The following oath is what they signed; now they took it together:

I, David Crockett Whitt, of the County of Tazewell, State of Virginia, do solemnly swear that I will support, protect, and defend the Constitution and Government of the United States against all enemies, whether domestic or foreign; that I will bear true faith, allegiance, and loyalty to the same, any ordinance, resolution, or laws of any State, Convention, or Legislature, to the contrary notwithstanding; and further, that I will faithfully perform all the duties which may be required of me by the laws of the United States; and I take this oath freely and voluntarily, without any mental reservation or evasion whatever.

Confederate American

Signed: David Crockett Whitt   Subscribed and sworn to before me, this 22nd day of June, 1865.

He (Major Brady) spoke a few words of thanks for them becoming United States Citizens again. Crockett and the men were jubilant, knowing that they were really going home. The sad thing was that some of the men were so sick and weak that they may not make it home. The night of the 21st one of the men died. The more healthy veterans helped the weaker men, and some would be helped all the way home by personal friends. After spending a day there without rations, there were enough men to make the trip on the 22nd of June, 1865.

Crockett and the others in the holding pen were ordered out; finally they would embark on the journey home as free men. They were loaded on one of those secondhand New York ferry boats. The men still had not been fed, but what was new about this place.

After arriving in Richmond, (Rocketts Landing) the men were met by some more Union soldiers. Here they were asked their destination and given a train passage from Richmond to the nearest train station to their home.

They complained that they had not been fed in two days, so the sergeant said he would see that they got a meal. They brought out crackers, a small portion of salt pork, and water. The men eat it savagely, and were glad to get it. Crockett took time to thank God for the food and for his new found freedom. He also asked God to go with each man, and get them home safely.

Colonel Charles Dahnmon Whitt

Hospital, thought to be at Lookout Point, Maryland.

Confederate American

Envelope Crockett's Letter came in.

Colonel Charles Dahnmon Whitt

> Point Lookout, May 30 '65
>
> Dear Father
>
> You will no doubt be surprised to receive a letter from me from this place. I arrived here 11" April was captured on the 6", near Farmville Va. I have signified my willingness to take the oath of allegiance. I wish you to go to work and try to get me released as soon as possible. I think if you make an effort you will be successful. I belonged to Co "H" 29" Va regt. If you can do nothing get my brother in law Thompson to do what he can. I have five comrades in here, if you can get them released by vouching for them I would like to have you do so. Their names are Burdell Brewster, J. W. Birchem, D. C. Lewis, Isaac Puckett, & Jas Colston all of my regt. Do what you can for me & write
>
> your aff son, David C. Whitt
> Prisoner of war Co D 7" Div Pt Lookout Md

This is a scan of the letter Crockett wrote to his father Jonas Whitt on May 30, 1865.

Confederate American

Point Lookout, Maryland, located in Saint Mary's County, Maryland on the southern tip of the peninsula was deemed the largest and worst Northern POW camp. Point Lookout was constructed of fourteen foot high wooden walls. These walls surrounded an area of about 40 acres. A walkway surrounded the top of the walls where Negro guards walked day and night. It is reported the guards were brutal in their treatment of prisoners. Prisoner, John R. King said; "Two days out of every three we were guarded by a gang of ignorant and cruelsome Negroes. Please do not think that I dislike the Negroes as a race. Many of them are my friends, but the Negroes authority over the white people and the defenseless prisoners suffered at their hands. Numbers of scars were left on the frame work of the closets made by Negroes firing at the prisoners. The negro guard was very insolent and delighted in tantalizing the prisoners, for some trifle affair, we were often accused of disobedience and they would say, *"Look out, white man, the bottom rail is on top now, so you had better be careful for my gun has been wanting to smoke at you all day!"*

No barracks were ever built. The Confederate soldiers were given tents to sleep in until overcrowding became so bad; there were not even enough tents to go around.

Approximately 50,000 Confederate enlisted men were contained within the walls of Point Lookout Prison Camp during its operation 1863-1865. Prison capacity was 10,000 but at any given time, there would be between 12,000 and 20,000 soldiers incarcerated there. The extreme overcrowding, Maryland's freezing temperatures, shortages of firewood for heat, and living in tents took its

Colonel Charles Dahnmon Whitt

toll and many lives were lost due to exposure. *The ratio of blankets to men was 1 blanket per 8 men!*

As the water supply became polluted and food rations ran low, prisoners died from disease and starvation. Food was in such short supply, the men were reported to hunt rats as a food source. A prisoner, Rev. J. B. Traywick said; *"Our suffering from hunger was indescribable"*. See more of his story at Treatment of Prisoners - Prison Life at Point Lookout.

Estimates report that over 14,000 prisoners died while imprisoned at Point Lookout but the cemetery is known to hold 3,384 soldiers in a mass grave with no evidence to back up this massive figure. According to history data received from Point Lookout State Park, "Of the 50,000 men held at the Point between 1863 and 1865, nearly 4,000 died. Ironically, however, this death rate of 8 percent was less than half the death rate among soldiers who were in the field with their own armies." As you can see, there seems to be some controversy over the number of deaths at this prison.

The Confederate soldiers' bodies have been moved twice and have found their final resting place in Point Lookout Cemetery.

The first Confederate monument ever constructed has been placed above this mass grave. Made of granite and standing over 85 feet tall, the base of it is covered with bronze tablets, telling the story of the Confederate soldiers lost at Point Lookout Civil War Prison.

The Point Lookout area is now known as Point Lookout State Park. A visitor's center and museum are located there. The museum contains photos of the POWs along

Confederate American

with some artifacts. If you are planning a visit there, look up **Point Lookout State Park.** Source: Reverend J.B. Traywick

This was the POW camp, (Point Lookout) that David Crockett Whitt, (My Great Grandfather, stayed at from the early part of April 1865 to June 22, 1865. I am lucky he made it out alive.

Colonel Charles Dahnmon Whitt

Chapter 10
Love for Lee and Jackson

Robert E. Lee

Confederate American

Robert Edward Lee (January 19, 1807 – October 12, 1870) was a career United States Army officer and combat engineer. He became the commanding general of the Confederate army in the American Civil War and a postwar icon of the South's "lost cause." A top graduate of West Point, Lee distinguished himself as an exceptional soldier in the U.S. Army for 32 years. He is best known for having commanded the Confederate Army of Northern Virginia in the American Civil War.

In early 1861, President Abraham Lincoln invited Lee to take command of the entire Union Army. Lee declined because his home state of Virginia was, despite his wishes, seceding from the Union. When Virginia declared its secession from the Union in April 1861, Lee chose to follow his home state. Lee's eventual role in the newly established Confederacy was to serve as a senior military adviser to President Jefferson Davis. Lee soon emerged as the shrewdest battlefield tactician of the war, after he assumed command of the Confederate eastern army (soon christened "The Army of Northern Virginia") after the wounding of Joseph Johnston at the Battle of Seven Pines. His abilities as a tactician were quickly made evident in his many victories such as the Battle of Fredericksburg (1862), Battle of Chancellorsville (1863), Battle of the Wilderness (1864) Battle of Cold Harbor (1864), Seven Days Battles, and the Second Battle of Bull Run. His strategic vision was more doubtful; his invasions of the North in 1862 and 1863 depended on the conviction that Northern morale was weak, hoping that a handful of rebel victories could shatter the North's willpower and possibly help to gain recognition and aid from European nations through negotiations. After a defeat at Antietam (1862) and disaster at Gettysburg (1863), hopes for

Colonel Charles Dahnmon Whitt

victory were dashed and defeat for the South was almost certain. However, due to ineffectual pursuit by the commander of Union forces, Lee escaped after both defeats to Virginia. His decision in 1863 to overrule his advisers and invade the North, rather than protect Vicksburg, proved a major strategic blunder and cost the Confederacy control of its western regions, nevertheless Lee's brilliant defensive maneuvers stopped the Union offenses one after another, as he defeated a series of Union commanders in Virginia.

In the spring of 1864, the new Union commander, Ulysses S. Grant, began a series of campaigns to wear down Lee's army. In the Overland Campaign of 1864 and the Siege of Petersburg in 1864–1865, Lee inflicted heavy casualties on Grant's larger army, but was forced back into trenches. The Confederacy was unable to replace his losses or even provide adequate rations to the soldiers that did not desert. In the final months of the Civil War, as manpower drained away, Lee adopted a plan to arm slaves to fight on behalf of the Confederacy, but the decision came too late and the black soldiers were never used in combat. In early April 1865, Lee's depleted forces were overwhelmed at Petersburg; he abandoned Richmond and retreated west as Union forces encircled his army. Lee surrendered to Grant at Appomattox Courthouse on April 9, 1865, marking the end of Confederate hopes. The remaining armies soon gave up and capitulated. Lee rejected the folly of starting a guerrilla campaign against the Yankees and called for reconciliation between the North and the South.

Lee's numerous victories against superior forces won him enduring fame as a crafty and daring battlefield tactician, but some of his strategic decisions, such as invading the

Confederate American

North in 1862 and 1863, have been criticized by many military historians.

After the war, as a college President, Lee supported President Andrew Johnson's program of Reconstruction and inter-sectional friendship while opposing the Radical Republican proposals to give freed slaves the vote and take the vote away from ex-Confederates. He urged them to re-think their position between the North and the South, and the reintegration of former Confederates into the nation's political life. Lee became the great Southern hero of the war and his popularity grew in the North as well after his death in 1870. He remains an iconic figure of American military leadership.   Source: Wikipedia the Free Encyclopedia

Robert Edward Lee

As we are entering a new century, we are enjoying prosperity and progress like never before. But even in light of this progress our hearts are turned to honor the memory of one Robert Edward Lee and as we face uncertain days for our heritage and our culture, we declare "we love you more than we ever did." Our ancestors who knew Lee and confederate information, who rode under his Generalship, who saw firsthand the effects of his leadership and character, saw the urgency and the importance of marking General Lee's birthday as a holiday. This holiday is to be kept as an opportunity and an obligation to tell succeeding generations of the greatness of this man and the enduring quality of the principles that he fought for. Today, we are gathered here with heads held high, voices uplifted and with hearts full in honor of one of God's greatest soldiers! General Robert Edward Lee.

Colonel Charles Dahnmon Whitt

There are certain reasons why Lee is today revered so highly; so much so that a news related poll two years ago noted that Lee is well over a century after his death in 1870, still the South's most revered figure. What characteristics of Lee so mark his greatness? Please allow me to give two choices made by our General that set him apart, yea, sanctify our General to a position of greatness among us.

Robert E. Lee was born into the famous Lee family of Virginia. Perhaps no extended family played a larger role in the founding of our Federal Republic than the Lee Family of Virginia. His father, "Light horse Harry" Lee was George Washington's closest friend and at Washington's funeral gave Washington the praise "first in war, first in peace and first in the hearts of his countrymen." Young Robert grew up with the desire to emulate George Washington. As a young man, Robert E. Lee won appointment to the US Military Academy where he finished near the top of his class, never receiving a demerit during his entire time as a Cadet. From there on, Robert E. Lee was the epitome of an all-American young man. He became a hero in the Mexican War and was named Superintendent of the US Military Academy. Now mind you, I am not just trying to recount his life to this point. I am hoping that you will understand when the crisis of secession came in 1861; Robert Edward Lee was considered a stellar American patriot. No military man had the leadership ability and confidence of fellow military men like Lee. This is evidenced by the fact that when the War began, Mr. Lincoln offered Robert E. Lee command of the Union forces. Please consider the scenario here. This young man had devoted his life to the service of the Union. He had trained to serve the military of the Union. His father and his uncles were part of the founding of this

Confederate American

Union. Now, his lifelong dream had been realized as he could follow the steps of his hero Washington as commander of the Union. This was the most agonizing choice Lee ever faced. Unlike the fire eaters like Edmund Ruffin, Robert Toombs and William Lowndes Yancey, Lee initially opposed secession, feeling it not the wisest immediate course. So, how could Lee ever turn down this magnificent offer?

Lee understood a deeper loyalty than loyalty to an organic Union. Lee understood that the highest loyalty is loyalty to the principle and Lee chose to follow the Constitution. Lee had studied Rawle's writings at West Point and had been nurtured at the breast of self-government under a Republican form of government. Lee correctly understood that secession was a right and that the Union was formed by the States. Thus, Lee's highest patriotic duty was with his native Virginia. Hear me today! While it may seem strange in our 21st Century to speak of secession, our founding fathers all understood that the states formed the Union, thus giving them a right to leave the Union. Lee understood that our Constitution is a compact among states and this was the prevailing view of most Americans during the first 80 years of our existence as a Republic. So, Lee had great sentiment with the Union, but he chose the Constitution and cast his lot with his highest loyalty, his home state of Virginia. Lee truly followed his hero George Washington by choosing the Constitution.

Robert Frost's poem The Road Less Traveled concludes with *"I took the road less traveled by, and that has made all the difference."* We are here today because Lee took the road less traveled by. He chose principle over expediency. Have you considered what would have

Colonel Charles Dahnmon Whitt

happened if Lee had taken Mr. Lincoln's offer? Well, for starters, he would have been the North's most brilliant officer and would likely have shortened the War. But Lee's greatness is not diminished due to providence determining that our side lost. Lee's choice was to do that which was right. Lee may have been made President of these United States, may have died a rich man but Lee made a choice that enabled him to die with a clear conscience. He stood for that which he knew to be right. We thrill at the Biblical stories of Daniel, cast in a den of lions, of little David and his defeat of the wicked giant Goliath with just a sling shot and the three Hebrew children who were cast into the fiery furnace, but yet protected by God. But there are other Biblical examples. John the Baptist was beheaded, early martyrs torn apart by lions and our Lord crucified on a tree. Right is not guaranteed to prevail in this life. Lee understood that he had no guarantee of earthly success, but he chose to do right by standing on the Constitution and in defense of his native Virginia.

Source: Michael Horton

General Lee loved his men and his men loved him. He was cheered by all the men that saw him. His men were dedicated to winning his battles and General Lee trusted them to do so.

The men loved the victories that General's Lee, and Jackson and other southern officers gave them. It was hard to believe that his men called him, "Granny Lee," when he first took command. He soon changed their minds with victory after victory.

Confederate American

Robert E. Lee

From "Harper's Weekly News Paper Saturday, July 2, 1864

Colonel Charles Dahnmon Whitt

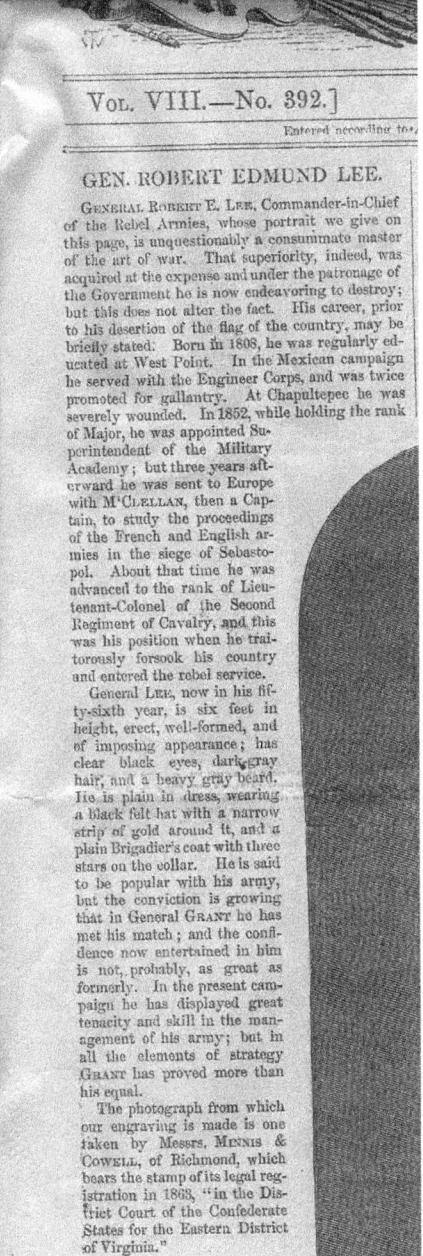

Negative review of "Bob Lee," by Harper's Weekly July 2, 1865

Confederate American

Measuring Robert E. Lee's greatness

Although his actual birthday is Jan. 19, Monday will be the day the state of Alabama observes the birthday of Gen. Robert E. Lee, a man about whom more has been written than any other American except George Washington. Not one writer, not one researcher, not one biographer has uncovered one stain on his character and morality.

Though his name inspired the hopes of hundreds of thousands of Southerners who never even saw him, his actual control was limited to 70,000 men of the Army of Northern Virginia, Confederate States Army.

Even today, his military tactics are studied at West Point. He was called the "Gray Fox" by Union commanders because of his ability to elude their much larger commands. The very best battlefield odds that Gen. Lee ever had were 4 to 1.

Robert E. Lee's leadership qualities are unsurpassed in American history. As he rode back from McLean House at Appomattox, his soldiers detected something different. The customary cheer froze in their throats and they began to ask, "General, are we surrendered?" Moving his lips in a choking "goodbye," he tried to ride on through.

"General, we'll fight 'em yet. General, say the word and we'll go in and fight 'em yet." Those words came from the throats of men whom Union soldiers describe as being so thin from starvation that they looked like scarecrows. But they stood there on dirty bare feet, begging to continue the fight.

They touched his uniform or his bridle rein if they could not grasp his hand; and if they could not reach him, they smoothed Traveler's flank or patted Traveler's neck.

Grim, bearded fellows who had stood in the trenches of Petersburg, gone through the Wilderness Campaign and withstood the fatal charge at Gettysburg, now battle-hardened veterans of four long years of combat, threw themselves on the ground, covered their faces and wept like children. Officers of all ranks made no attempt to conceal their feelings, either, but sat on their horses and wept aloud.

After Appomattox, as Gen. Lee and his small party made their way into the streets of Richmond, the city he had defended for four long years, federal soldiers were already occupying the former capital of the Confederacy. No one knew better than they how great a general was passing and what it had taken to bleed his army to death.

Block after block, these federal soldiers in blue raised their caps and held them high, honoring the man they wished had ridden with them instead of against them.

And being the gentleman that he was, Gen. Lee raised his muddy wide-brimmed hat, inclining his head politely each time he did so. It was his last parade, and he wished it over.

In 1868, the New York Herald said this about Robert E. Lee: "With a handful of men whom he molded into an army, he battled our greater Northern armies for four years, and when opposed by Grant was only worn down by that solid strategy of stupidity that accomplishes its object by mere weight.

"With one-quarter of the men Grant had, this soldier fought magnificently across his native state, and fought his army to a stump. There was never such an army or such a campaign or such a general."

Let us remember that winning is not always the measure of greatness.

ELLEN WILLIAMS
Leroy

Clipping from Mobile, AL. Newspaper January 2005

Colonel Charles Dahnmon Whitt

Stonewall Jackson, Lee's Right Arm
Thomas Jonathan Jackson

(January 21, 1824 to May 10, 1863)

Stonewall Jackson (January 21, 1824 to May 10, 1863) was a Confederate general during the American Civil War, and probably the most well-known Confederate commander after General Lee. His military career includes the Valley Campaign of 1862 and his service as a corps commander in the Army of Northern Virginia under Robert E. Lee. Confederate pickets accidentally shot him at the Battle of Chancellorsville on May 2, 1863, which the general survived, albeit with the loss of an arm to amputation. However, he died of complications of pneumonia eight days later. His death was a severe

Confederate American

setback for the Confederacy, affecting not only its military prospects, but also the morale of its army and of the general public.

Military historians consider Jackson to be one of the most gifted tactical commanders in United States history. His Valley Campaign and his envelopment of the Union Army right wing at Chancellorsville are studied worldwide even today as examples of innovative and bold leadership. He excelled as well in other battles: the First Battle of Bull Run (where he received his famous nickname "Stonewall"), Second Bull Run, Antietam, and Fredericksburg. Jackson was not universally successful as a commander however, as displayed by his weak and confused efforts during the Seven Days Battles around Richmond in 1862.

He entered West Point in July 1842 and in spite of his poor childhood education, worked hard to graduate seventeenth in his class in 1846. Upon graduation Jackson was sent on military duty to Mexico. He continued his service in the United States Army in positions in New York and Florida. In 1851, Jackson became professor of artillery tactics and natural philosophy at Virginia Military Institute in Lexington, Virginia.

On May 2, 1863, in his last march of the Civil War, Jackson was wounded by friendly fire. He died of pneumonia several days later on May 10 at Guiney's Station, Virginia. His body was carried to Richmond and then to Lexington where it was buried.

Colonel Charles Dahnmon Whitt

It is said that The Army of Northern Virginia never fully recovered from the loss of Stonewall Jackson's leadership during the remainder of the War of Northern Aggression. This writing views Jackson by art and culture rather than military or political aspects. This somewhat calm, domestic period in his life came to a close on April 21, 1861 when he was ordered to go to Richmond as part of the cadet corps. Since military aspirations had faded from his life, he was virtually unknown in the military world.

It was during the Battle of Bull Run in the Civil War when Jackson assumed his nickname. Amidst the tumult of battle, Brigadier-General Barnard E. Bee stated, "There is Jackson standing like a stone wall." As the war continued, Jackson continually impressed his Confederate compatriots with his skill on the battlefield and in planning conferences. He distinguished himself in the Valley campaign of early 1862, the Battle of second Manassas in August 1862, and the Battle of Fredericksburg in December 1862. Jackson was a Southern hero and in spite of his eccentricities, he was loved and respected by his soldiers. He strictly observed the Sabbath and his love of God was constant in all facets of his life. General Jackson never feared death; he was a devout Christian and reasoned he would live until God called him home. Had Jackson lived, who knows what may have happened.

Sources: Dictionary of American Biography and Wikipedia the Free Encyclopedia

Confederate American

FUNERAL PROCESSION IN HONOR OF LIEUT. GEN. Thomas J. JACKSON

The funeral procession which yesterday took place in token of regard for the lamented Jackson afforded the best evidence of the high estimation in which the deceased was held by the country which is now called to mourn over his death.

On Monday night the remains of the lamented chieftain were embalmed, and about 11 o'clock, yesterday, in pursuance of public announcement, were taken from the mansion of the Governor, through several of the main thoroughfares of the city, to the Capitol, where they were laid in state, and were viewed for the last time by his many friends and admirers. Long before the appointed hour for the procession to move a dense crowd had congregated on the Square to pay the last sad tribute of respect to one who all delighted to honor. The solemn tolling of the bells and the firing of minute guns gave notice that the ceremonies were about to commence, and at 11 o'clock, in obedience to an order of Major General Elzey, the body, which had been placed in a metallic burial-case, was removed from the reception room of the Governor's mansion and placed in a hearse in attendance. The procession then took up the line of march down Governor Street.

These were followed by a large number of military and civil dignitaries, mounted and on foot. The route of the

Colonel Charles Dahnmon Whitt

procession was down Governor street to Main, up Main to Second, up Second to Grace, and down Grace to the West gate of the Capitol Square, where all entered except the military escort, which filed up 9th street.

On arriving at the Capitol the coffin containing the remains of the lamented hero, borne by the bearers, was conveyed to the large hall in the Southern end of the building, and the doors thrown open to afford an opportunity to the eager crowd to look upon the features of one whose death they regarded as a great national calamity. Good order was observed, and the dense crowd slowly made its way through the rotunda into the large hall where the coffin laid, and as they passed gazed for the last time upon all that is mortal of the gallant dead.

Many of the ladies, as they passed, shed tears over the remains, and, in token of their deep regard for the memory of the noble chieftain, pressed their lips upon the lid of his coffin. Witnessing the deep feeling of sorrow manifested by these fair daughters of Virginia, an elderly and respectable-looking gentleman addressed them in tones of condolence, as follows: "Weep not; all is for the best. Though Jackson has been taken from the head of his corps, his spirit is now pleading our cause at the bar of God."

For hours after the coffin had been placed in the large hall thousands continued to crowd in and around the Capitol, awaiting their turn for a last look at the features fixed in death. – The coffin which contained the remains of the deceased was a metallic one, with glass door over the face. On the coffin was a silver plate, upon which was engraved the simple inscription:

Confederate American

"Lieutenant-General T. J. Jackson. Born January 21st, 1824; died May 10, 1863." All the incidents connected with these interesting, but melancholy ceremonies, were marked by a deep feeling of sorrow. Eyes unused to weep were suffused with tears, and the great popular heart pulsated with emotions of grief too deep for utterance.

It is understood that the remains of the deceased will this morning be conveyed from the Capitol of Virginia to his late home, Lexington, Rockbridge County, where they will be interred.

Richmond Daily Dispatch, page 1   5/13/1863   Wednesday,

Colonel Charles Dahnmon Whitt
Chapter 11
Tricks of War

Desperate times require desperate measures, and in warfare few are more cunning or dangerous than the desperate. Although the Federals did manage to pull off their fair share, it was the Confederates who were responsible for the majority of the hoaxes that were perpetrated during the Civil War. This stands to reason considering the Confederate's predicament. Desperately lacking in both men and materiel, Confederate commanders were often forced to resort to correspondingly desperate measures, such as deception, in order to mask or offset those deficiencies. Some, including famed cavalryman Nathan Bedford Forrest, would even attain near legendary status for their seemingly magician like talents.

It was Thomas J. "Stonewall" Jackson, however, who best defined the Confederate tricksters' creed when he wrote, *"Always mystify, mislead, and surprise the enemy."*

Confederate American

The Quaker Gun below was found near Centreville, Virginia, in March 1862, after the Confederate withdrawal.

Quaker Guns were usually painted black, used to trick an enemy. Misleading the enemy as to the strength of cannons and man power was an effective delaying tactic. The name derives from the Religious Society of Friends called "Quakers", who have traditionally held a religious opposition to war and violence in the Peace Testimony and used these false weapons to intimidate possible foes without breaching their pacifistic vows.

A **Quaker Gun, (Dummy Gun)** is a deceptive trick that was commonly used in warfare during the 18th and 19th centuries. Although resembling an actual cannon, the Quaker Gun (Dummy Gun) was simply a wooden log.

Colonel Charles Dahnmon Whitt
The original "Quaker Gun trick"

During the American War of Independence, after nearly a year of brutal backcountry conflict between American Colonel William Washington and the fierce British commander Lieutenant Colonel Banastre Tarleton, Colonel Washington had retreated to North Carolina in October 1780.

Ordered to return to lead an irregular force of colonial soldiers in the South Carolina theater by Brigadier General Daniel Morgan, Colonel Washington still lacked the proper artillery to dislodge the Loyalists. On December 4, the Americans were able to trap the Loyalist Colonel Rowland Rugeley and his company of men estimated to be about 125 in Rugeley's house and barn near Camden, South Carolina. He told his cavalrymen to dismount and surround the barn. While out of Rugeley's sight, Washington's men fabricated a pine log to resemble a cannon. Where Washington got the idea I don't know.

This so called "Quaker Gun Trick" worked wonderfully. Colonel Washington faced the fake cannon toward the buildings in which the Loyalists had barricaded themselves and threatened bombardment if they did not surrender. Shortly afterwards, Rugeley surrendered his entire force without a single shot being fired.

Confederate American

Used during the American Civil War

Quaker guns made of pine logs were mounted in a likely frame to fool the Union into believing that the Confederates were much better armed at the Siege of Port Hudson, Louisiana in 1863. Black rings were painted on the end of the logs to make the muzzles look convincing. It worked. After Admiral Farragut's two vessels passed by Port Hudson, the Union chose to never attack from the river again.

Quaker guns were used by both the Union and Confederates in the American Civil War. The Confederate States Army frequently used them to compensate for a shortage of artillery. They were painted black at the muzzle, and positioned behind fortifications to delay Union assaults on those positions. On occasion, real gun carriages were used to complete the trickery.

Perhaps the most famous use of Quaker Guns was by Confederate General Joseph E. Johnston. The General had the dummy guns put in his field works around

Colonel Charles Dahnmon Whitt

Centreville, Virginia in March 1862, This made the Union think the works were still occupied while, in fact, the Confederates were withdrawing to the Rappahannock River.

Another major example occurred during the Siege of Corinth: "During the night of May 29, the Confederate army moved out. They used the Mobile and Ohio Railroad to carry the sick and wounded the heavy artillery, and tons of supplies. When a train arrived, the troops cheered as though reinforcements were arriving. They set up dummy Quaker Guns along the defensive earthworks. Camp fires were kept burning, and buglers and drummers played. The rest of the men slipped away undetected. It was a perfect trick.

The old adage of, "All is fair in love and war," was kept by both the Confederates and the Union. It was alright to deceive the enemy, but honor forbid out right lying.

Nathan Bedford Forrest was a resourceful General, by using his tactics General Nathan Bedford Forrest took more than 1,400 Union soldiers prisoner when he tricks Col. Wallace Campbell into surrendering a fort on Coleman Hill near Athens. Forrest convinced Campbell that his force was three times its actual size and that resisting or waiting on reinforcements was pointless. Most of the Union troops were from the 110th U.S. Colored Infantry, which was made up of former slaves from northern Alabama and southern Tennessee.

General Forrest also pulled the same trick on Colonel Abel D. Streight in March of 1863. Through trickery Forest convinced Streight that he was highly out numbered. Streight surrendered his whole command of over 1,500 men while Forrest only had slightly over 600 men.

Confederate American

General Nathan Bedford Forrest was a slick commander that should have been utilized more in General Lee's army.

Born July 23, 1821 in Tennessee

General Nathan Bedford Forrest
It was reported that Forrest had several Black Soldiers with him and eight of his slaves rode with him fully armed.

Colonel Charles Dahnmon Whitt
Chapter 12

Black Confederates

Did blacks fight in combat for the Confederacy?

One of the more interesting questions related to blacks serving in the American Civil War is this, **did blacks (free or slave) serve in combat roles in the Confederate Army?** Unquestionably the historical evidence is strong that some blacks, perhaps several thousand, did serve in the Confederate Army in unofficial, noncombatant roles as servants, laborers, teamster, musician, cooks, etc.

Confederate American

But the official record is very unsupportive that thousands of blacks served as official soldiers in the ranks of the Southern soldiers' rosters.

When we use the word official we mean that a black soldier would have been documented through the same paperwork process as a white man would have in terms of enlisting, mustering in or out, and perhaps applying for pension benefits after the war. It is this logistical paperwork process that leaves a trail for historians to study and interpret.

How strong is the historical evidence such as letters, diaries, first-hand accounts, military records, which blacks served in combat roles as Confederate soldiers? It is an important question.

Besides the fact that it is important to preserve accurate history it is also important to "get it right" when it comes to knowing who fought in the Civil War so that these individuals can be properly honored and their place in history duly noted. Some who favor a Southern perspective on the war, particularly defending the proposition that the South did not fight to preserve or defend slavery, have argued that thousands of slaves fought on behalf of the South thereby proving that they were generally supportive of the Southern way of life.

Black Confederates? Why haven't we heard more about them? National Park Service historian, Ed Bearrs, stated, "I don't want to call it a conspiracy to ignore the role of Blacks both above and below the Mason-Dixon line, but it was definitely a tendency that began around 1910" Historian, Erwin L. Jordan, Jr., calls it a "cover-up" which

Colonel Charles Dahnmon Whitt

started back in 1865. He writes, "During my research, I came across instances where black men stated they were soldiers, but you can plainly see where the word *"soldier"* is crossed out and the word *"body servant"* inserted, or *"teamster"* on pension applications." Another black historian, Roland Young, says he is not surprised that blacks fought. He explains that, *"some, if not most, black southerners would support their country"* and that by doing so they were, *"demonstrating it's possible to hate the system of slavery and love one's country."* This is the very same reaction that most African Americans showed during the American Revolution, where they fought for the colonies, even though the British offered them freedom if they fought for them.

It has been estimated that over 65,000 Southern blacks were in the Confederate ranks. Over 13,000 of these, "saw the elephant" also known as meeting the enemy in combat. These Black Confederates included both slave and free. The Confederate Congress did not approve blacks to be officially enlisted as soldiers (except as musicians), until late in the war.

But in the ranks it was a different story. Many Confederate officers did not obey the mandates of politicians, they frequently enlisted blacks with the simple criteria with, and "Will you fight?"

Historian Ervin Jordan, explains that *"biracial units"* were frequently organized *"by local Confederate and State militia Commanders in response to immediate threats in the form of Union raids"*. Dr. Leonard Haynes, an African American professor at Southern University, stated, *"When you eliminate the black Confederate soldier, you've eliminated the history of the South."*

As the war came to an end, the Confederacy took

Confederate American

progressive measures to build back up its army. The creation of the Confederate States Colored Troops, copied after the segregated northern colored troops, came too late to be successful. Had the Confederacy been successful, it would have created the world's largest armies (at the time) consisting of black soldiers, even larger than that of the North. This would have given the future of the Confederacy a vastly different appearance than what modern day racist or anti-Confederate liberals conjecture. Not only did Jefferson Davis envision black Confederate veterans receiving bounty lands for their service, there would have been no future for slavery after the goal of 300,000 armed black CSA veterans came home after the war.

Source: Scott K. Williams

Colonel Charles Dahnmon Whitt

Picture of an unknown Black Confederate

About Blacks Who Fought For the South

Most historical accounts portray Southern blacks as anxiously awaiting President Abraham Lincoln's "liberty-dispensing troops" marching south in the War Between the States. But there's more to the story; let's look at it.

Confederate American

Black Confederate military units, both as freemen and slaves, fought federal troops. Louisiana free blacks gave their reason for fighting in a letter written to New Orleans' Daily Delta: "The free colored populations love their home, their property, and their own slaves and recognize no other country than Louisiana and are ready to shed their blood for her defense. They have no sympathy for Abolitionism; no love for the North, but they have plenty for Louisiana. They will fight for her in 1861 as they fought in 1814-15." As to bravery, one black scolded the commanding general of the state militia, saying, "Pardon me, general, but the only cowardly blood we have got in our veins is the white blood."

Gen. Nathan Bedford Forrest had slaves and freemen serving in units under his command. After the war, Forrest said of the black men who served under him, "These boys stayed with me and better Confederates did not live." Articles in "Black Southerners in Gray," edited by Richard Rollins, gives numerous accounts of blacks serving as fighting men or servants in every battle from Gettysburg to Vicksburg.

Professor Ed Smith, director of American Studies at American University, says Stonewall Jackson had 3,000 fully equipped black troops scattered throughout his corps at Antietam, the war's bloodiest battle. Mr. Smith calculates that between 60,000 and 93,000 blacks served the Confederacy in some capacity. They fought for the same reason they fought in previous wars and wars afterward: "to position themselves. They had to prove they were patriots in the hope the future would be better ...

Colonel Charles Dahnmon Whitt

they hoped to be rewarded."

Many knew Lincoln had little love for enslaved blacks and didn't wage war against the South for their benefit. Lincoln made that plain, saying, "I will say, then, that I am not, nor have ever been in favor of bringing about in any way the social and political equality of the white and black races I am in favor of having the superior position assigned to the white race." The very words of his 1863 Emancipation Proclamation revealed his deceit and cunning; it freed those slaves held "within any State or designated part of a State the people whereof shall then be in rebellion against the United States." It didn't apply to slaves in West Virginia and areas and states not in rebellion. Like General Ulysses Grant's slaves, they had to wait for the 13th Amendment.

Grant explained why he didn't free his slaves earlier, saying, "Good help is so hard to come by these days."

Lincoln waged war to "preserve the Union". The 1783 peace agreement with England (Treaty of Paris] left 13 sovereign nations. They came together in 1787, as principals, to create a federal government, as their agent, giving it specific delegated authority specified in our Constitution. Principals always retain the right to fire their agent. When The Southerners fired on Fort Sumter, U.S. Government property, this gave Lincoln the excuse he needed to wage war

The War Between the States, through force of arms, settled the question of secession, enabling the federal government to run roughshod over states' rights specified by the Constitution's 10th Amendment.

Sons of Confederate Veterans are a group dedicated to giving a truer account of the War Between the States. I'd

Confederate American

like to see it erect on Richmond's Monument Avenue a statue of one of the thousands of black Confederate soldiers.

Source: This article appeared in the Washington Times some years back. It was written by Walter Williams

Documents of Lincoln's Racism

Abraham Lincoln "was a racist who opposed equal Rights for black people, who loved minstrel shows, Who used the Nigger word, who wanted to deport All blacks," a veteran journalist and historian says. "There has been a systematic attempt to keep the American public from knowing the real Lincoln and The depth of his commitment to white supremacy," Says Lerone Bennett Jr.,

Colonel Charles Dahnmon Whitt

Chapter 13

Confederate Doctors

Confederate Medical Department

The following statement is quoted from an address by S. P. Moore, M.D., surgeon-general of the Confederate States army, delivered at Richmond, Virginia, October 19, 1875:

"Congressional Legislation. To make the corps still more effective, to hold out rewards to distinguished medical officers, to offer incentives (if needed) to faithful and efficient performance of duties, and to confer additional and commensurate authority on those in most important positions, a bill was prepared creating the offices of two assistant surgeon-generals, one to exercise authority west of the Mississippi, the other to be on duty in the surgeon general's office; medical directors, medical inspectors, medical purveyors, all with rank of colonel. This bill passed both Houses of Congress (they appearing willing always to aid the department in its effort toward a more perfect organization), but was vetoed by the President. It seemed useless to make further efforts in this direction."

To each regiment of infantry or cavalry was assigned a surgeon and an assistant surgeon; to a battalion of either, and sometimes to a company of artillery, an assistant surgeon. Whenever regiments and battalions were combined into brigades, the surgeon whose commission bore the oldest date became the senior surgeon of brigade, and although a member of the staff of the brigade commander, was not relieved of his regimental duties;

Confederate American

sometimes, however, he was allowed an additional assistant surgeon, who was carried on the brigade roster. To the senior surgeon of brigade, the regimental and battalion medical officers made their daily morning, weekly, monthly, and quarterly reports, and reports of killed and wounded after engagements, which by him were consolidated and forwarded to the chief surgeon of the division to which the brigade was attached; regiments and brigades acting in an independent capacity forwarded their reports to the medical director of the army or department, or to the surgeon general direct. Requisitions for regimental and battalion medical, surgical, and hospital supplies, as well as applications for furlough or leave of absence, discharge, resignation, or assignment to post duty, on account of disability, were first approved by the regimental or battalion medical officer, after giving his reasons for approval and the nature of the disability in the latter instances, and forwarded by him to the senior surgeon of brigade, and by him to the chief surgeon of division and the other ranking officers in the corps and army for their approval. Independent commands reported to the medical director of the department or army, or the surgeon general direct. Medical purveyors nearest to the army, as promptly as possible, forwarded all needed medical, surgical and hospital supplies, on approved requisitions.

Assignments to the position of chief surgeon of division were sometimes made in accordance with seniority of rank of the senior surgeons of brigades, in other instances on application of the general commanding the division. His duties, in addition to approving reports coming from the senior surgeons of brigades, were to advise with the division commander in all matters pertaining to the

Colonel Charles Dahnmon Whitt

medical care and hygiene of his command, and to have personal care of the attaches of the division staff and headquarters, and to advise and consult with his medical subordinates. To each corps was assigned a medical director, a commissioned surgeon, his permanent assignment being made on personal application of the lieutenant-general commanding the corps; temporarily and when emergency demanded, his duties, which were similar to those of the chief surgeon of division as pertaining to the corps, devolved upon the chief surgeon of division whose commission bore priority of date; he, in turn, being succeeded by the ranking senior surgeon of brigade.

A medical director was assigned to the staff of each general commanding a department, or an army in a department, his selection usually being in deference to the general on whose staff he served and to whom was submitted for approval all reports and papers, from the various army corps, independent divisions, brigades, or smaller detachments. He also had charge of the staff and attaches of the department or army headquarters.

The non commissioned medical staff consisted of a hospital steward for each regiment or battalion, with the rank and emoluments of an orderly sergeant, his selection as a rule being made by the ranking medical officer of the command, usually a graduate or undergraduate in medicine, or one having had previous experience in handling drugs; and his duties were to have charge of the medical, surgical, and hospital supplies under direction of the regimental or battalion medical officer, caring for and dispensing the same, seeing that the directions of his superior as to diet and medicines were carried out, or reporting their neglect or failure. The regimental band constituted the infirmary detail to aid in caring for the sick

Confederate American

in camp and to carry the wounded from the field of battle, and when so occupied were under the surgeon or assistant surgeon. When necessary, additional detail was made from the enlisted men to serve temporarily or permanently on the infirmary corps. In some instances, an enlisted man was detailed as hospital clerk, and with the hospital steward was required to be present at sick-call each morning; these soldiers, with the infirmary detail, were relieved from all other regimental duty, such as guard duty and police detail.

The duties of the surgeons, in addition to caring for the sick in camp and on the march, were to establish a field hospital, as soon as they could learn that the command to which they were attached was going under fire, at some convenient and, if possible, sheltered spot behind a hill or in a ravine, about one-half to one mile in rear of the line of battle, which was done under direction of a brigade or division surgeon. Here the combined medical staff of a brigade or division aided one another in the performance of such operations as were deemed necessary. As the wounded were brought from the front by the infirmary detail on stretchers or in the ambulance. Amputations, resections of bone, ligatures of arteries, removals of foreign bodies, adjusting and permanently fixing fractures, and all minor and major operations and dressings were made when deemed best for the comfort and welfare of the wounded men. As soon as possible after the permanent dressings were made at the field hospital and even in some instances while the troops were still engaged, the wounded were carried to the railroad and transported to the more permanent hospitals in the villages, towns, and cities, some miles distant.

Colonel Charles Dahnmon Whitt

The uniform worn by the medical corps was similar to that of the rank and file with only a slight difference. While the cloth and cut were the same, the facings of the coat collar and cuffs and the stripe down the sides of the trousers were black, while those of the infantry were light blue, the artillery, scarlet, and cavalry, buff. On the front of the cap or hat were the letters "M. S." embroidered in gold, embraced in two olive branches. On the coat sleeve of the assistant surgeon were two rows of gold braid, with three gold bars on the ends of the coat collar extending back about one and a half inches; while the surgeon had three rows of braid on the coat sleeves, and a single star on each side of the coat collar about an inch and a half from the end. The chevrons on the coat sleeves and the stripe down the trousers of the hospital steward were similar to those worn by an orderly or first sergeant, but were black in color.

The statement is sometimes made that many Confederate surgeons were inefficient, and in support of this contention a statement attributed to President Davis, in Surgeon Craven's "Prison Life of Jefferson Davis " is produced, in which he is reported to have said in conversation with the author, that " *they had been obliged to accept as surgeons in the Southern army many lads who had only half finished their education in Northern colleges.*"

This statement would seem to indicate a scarcity of capable medical men who were willing to serve as such in the Confederate army, While the facts are that many of the infantry and cavalry battalions and regiments, as well as artillery companies, in addition to their usual complement of medical officers, bore on their rolls, either in field and staff, the commissioned officers of the line, or even in rank and file, capable and eminently well qualified medical men, many of whom were subsequently

Confederate American

transferred to the medical corps. The reports from Northern prisons where line officers or enlisted men often assisted the Federal surgeons in the care of the sick, confirm this statement.

It can be said, in all sincerity and confidence in the statement, that the students of the South, who graduated from Northern and Southern medical colleges prior to the War Between the States, were superior in scholastic attainments and mental qualifications to those of subsequent years. Not only is this the personal observation of the writer. The following quotations were from an address by Samuel H. Stout, M.D., late medical director of hospitals of the Department and Army of Tennessee.

"When I attended lectures in Philadelphia more than half a century ago, the number of students in the two schools there (the University, and the Jefferson) was a little more than one thousand, more than half of whom were from the Southern States. Of these latter, a majority was Bachelors of Arts, or had received a classical education. The Southern States in the slaveholding sections were, therefore, prior to the war well supplied with educated and chivalrously honorable surgeons and physicians. Such were the men who served at the bedside and in responsible positions in the medical corps of the armies and navy of the Confederacy."

Finally, Samuel P. Moore, M.D., in an address delivered at Richmond, Virginia, October 19, 1865, published in the city papers of the following day, said, *"The Confederate medical officers were inferior to none in any army"*; and in another paragraph: "Although there were *many capital*

Colonel Charles Dahnmon Whitt

medical men in the medical corps, yet, from the easy manner by which commissions were obtained for medical officers appointed to regiments, many were supposed not to be properly qualified. It was therefore deemed advisable to establish army medical boards for the examination of medical officers already in service, as well as applicants for commission into the medical corps. These boards were to hold plain, practical examinations. The result was highly satisfactory."

In Tennessee, more than one instance can be mentioned where a good and well qualified practitioner, on application to Governor Harris for a position in the medical corps, was by him urgently and earnestly advised and entreated to remain at home, as be would be needed there, because, as quite a number of his colleagues were to be found in the rank and file of the assembling as soldiers, in addition to a full complement in the medical corps, the old men, the women and children, and the slaves at home must be cared for as well as the "boys" in the army. This measure prevailed in other States, and in only a few instances of rare emergency that could not by any means have been avoided, and then only for a brief period, was there any dearth or scarcity of medical officers in the Confederate army, in the field or hospital.

Some States began organizing their troops before affiliating with the Confederacy, as in Tennessee. The medical officers received their commissions from the secretary of state, after examinations, both oral and written, by an army medical examining board appointed by the governor of the State. The medical examining board at Nashville was headed by Dr. Paul F. Eve, a teacher of surgery of wide experience, and a surgeon of both national and international reputation. His colleagues were Dr. Joseph Newman, who bad served with the

Confederate American

Tennessee troops in the war with Mexico, and enjoyed the confidence and esteem of a large clientele in Nashville during the intervening years, and Dr. J. D. Winston, also one of the leading practitioners of the capital city of the State. Boards of like character were serving the western division of the State at Memphis, and at Knoxville, in the eastern. When the State troops, then organized, were transferred to the Confederate States, they were re-commissioned by the Secretary of War of the Confederacy, on recommendation of the surgeon general, after examination and approval by the army medical examining boards of the Confederate army. As other troops were subsequently organized, they were supplied with medical officers who had passed a satisfactory examination before a Confederate army medical examining board and commissioned in like manner. The same measure was followed in the hospital service.

The examinations before State and Confederate Army boards were thorough, complete, and eminently practical. Each applicant was required in a given number of hours to fill out the answers to a number of written questions, under supervision of the secretary of the board; and this being done; he was invited into an adjoining room and submitted to an oral examination to the satisfaction of the assembled board. The Confederate board of examiners serving with the Department and Army of Tennessee, as I remember, consisted of Dr. D. W. Yandell, of Louisville; Dr. J. F. Heustis, of Mobile, and Dr. Stanford E. Chaille, of New Orleans, all being well known teachers of medicine and surgery in their respective States, and at that time, or subsequently, of national reputation. Other medical examining boards were of like character.

Colonel Charles Dahnmon Whitt

The late Doctor Chaille, the dean of the medical department of Tulane University, in a private letter, speaks of the work of the examining boards appointed in 1862 to report on the competency of the medical staff. The Confederate soldiers were almost exclusively volunteers who had elected their medical as well as other officers. Doctor Chaille reported that his board caused the dismissal of a number of the surgeons and assistant surgeons, sometimes incurring the hostility of the officers and men in consequence, *"because of the gross incompetence of laymen then* as well as now *to judge of the incompetence of medical men."* He goes on to say that the incompetent were "exceptions to the superior merit of the vast majority of the members of the Confederate medical staff." This statement goes far to explain any apparent contradictions in the testimony regarding the competence of Confederate surgeons, and must be generally accepted.

Source: "The Photographic History of the Civil War" Volume IV, article by Deering J. Roberts, M.D., Surgeon, Confederate States Army

There were so many bones shattered by the "Minnie Balls," and "Grape Shot" which led to so many amputations.

The following statement is quoted from an address by S. P. Moore, M.D., surgeon-general of the Confederate States army, delivered at Richmond, Virginia, October 19, 1875:

Confederate American

"More about Confederate Doctors."

Posted by: Dr. James Jones

We hear many complaints of the medical staff of our army. Some skillful and careful physicians have gone out with the regiments: of them we desire to speak with all respect. They are doing much for humanity and their country. If disease attacks camps and kills more soldiers than bullets, then doctors are as important as generals, who maneuver the soldiers in the face of an enemy. But when the volunteers start for the wars, they are healthy and buoyant, and don't feel like they will ever need a physician. It is not thought of much consequence then who the surgeon is; and if some physician out of practice, and of no force beyond being a clever fellow, offers, he is elected. But when disease begins to prey on the ranks, then they often need a different man from the one who moves about them, with cap and lace. "No private soldier," said one of these wasted forms to us -- "no private soldier can get any attention from the surgeons in half the regiments. Go to him when you are sick, he will curse round a while, and tell you go back to your tent and he will come and see you directly, and that is the last of it." A contemporary, who has had a look into camp, says:

"From what we are able to learn, some of the hospital are poorly managed. Some are dirty and filthy enough to make a well man sick, and of course not a fit place at all for a sick man to regain his health.

"A humbug, mountebank doctor, who knows nothing, and who is good for nothing but to drink up the liquor provided for the sick, ought never to be allowed about a camp or

Colonel Charles Dahnmon Whitt

hospital.

"It is said that an upstart surgeon, who goes about the camps with a stone heart in his breast, is more dreaded by the soldiers after a battle than the enemy's weapons are before it. Men can't afford to lose an arm or a leg, and such members should be should not be amputated if there is any chance to restore them or heal the wound. The cutting and carving of flesh and bones is horrible, and a careful investigation should be made in every instance before the knife is resorted to."
Christian Advocate.
Nashville Daily Gazette, December 6, 1861

Confederate American

Union medical personnel picking up their wounded in blankets after the battle of Pittsburg Landing in Tennessee. Sketch by Henri Lovie 1862

Colonel Charles Dahnmon Whitt

Chapter 14
Rebel Yell

Confederate Soldiers Charge at the Battle of Shiloh

The **rebel yell** was a battle cry used by Confederate soldiers during the American Civil War. Confederate soldiers would use the yell during charges to intimidate the enemy and boost their own morale, although the yell had other uses. The exact sound of the yell is unknown and the subject of much speculation and debate. Likewise, the origin of the yell is uncertain.

Units were nicknamed for their apparent ability to yell during battle. The 35th Battalion of Virginia Cavalry "White's Cavalry" was given the sound of "Comanches" for the way they sounded during battle.

The sound of the yell has been the subject of much discussion and debate. Civil War soldiers, upon hearing

Confederate American

the yell from afar, would quip that it was either "Jackson, or a rabbit," suggesting a similarity between the sound of the yell and a rabbit's scream. The rebel yell has also been likened to the scream of a "Wild Cat". In media such as movies or video games, the yell is often portrayed as a simple "yee-haw" and in some parts of the United States, "yee-ha". The yell has also been described as similar to Native American cries. One description says it was a cross between an "Indian whoop and wolf-howl".

Though hardly a definitive description, having been published some 70 years after the war ended, Margaret Mitchell's classic Civil War novel *Gone with the Wind* has a character giving the yell sounding as a "yee-aay-eee" upon hearing the war had started. The film version, by contrast, has the yell sounding as a high pitched "yay-hoo" repeated several times in rapid succession.

Several recordings of possibly accurate yells exist. One, from a newsreel documenting the 75th anniversary of the Battle of Gettysburg, documents several Confederate veterans performing the yell as a high-pitched "Wa-woo-woohoo, wa-woo woohoo."

Given the differences in descriptions of the yell, there may have been several distinctive yells associated with the different regiments and their respective geographical areas.

In Ken Burns's documentary *The Civil War*, Shelby Foote notes that historians aren't quite sure how the yell sounded, being described as *"a foxhunt yip mixed up with sort of a banshee squall"*. He recounts the story of an old Confederate veteran invited to speak before a ladies'

Colonel Charles Dahnmon Whitt

society dinner. They asked him for a demonstration of the rebel yell, but he refused on the grounds that it could only be done "at a run", and couldn't be done anyway with "a mouth full of false teeth and a belly full of food". Antidotes from former Union Soldiers described the yell with reference to "a peculiar corkscrew sensation that went up your spine when you heard it" along with a claim that *"if you claim you heard it and weren't scared that means you never heard it".*

In his autobiography *My Own Story*, Bernard Baruch recalls how his father, a former surgeon in the Confederate army, would at the sound of the song "Dixie" jump up and give the rebel yell, no matter where he was. "As soon as the tune started Mother knew what was coming and so did we boys. Mother would catch him by the coattails and plead, *"Shush, Doctor, shush."* But it never did any good. I have seen Father, ordinarily a model of reserve and dignity, leap up in the Metropolitan Opera House and let loose that piercing yell."

From Wikipedia, the free encyclopedia

More about the *Rebel Yell*

One of the most enduring legends of the American Civil War is that of the *'Rebel Yell'* we hear a great deal about it, though no two people seem agreed on the sound, or even on its origin. What did it sound like? Was it the same through the country? It's definite that the sound was different than that shouted by Federal troops *"...their peculiar, characteristic yell (was)...Hoo-ray! Hoo-ray! Hoo-*

Confederate American

ray!" called by the Federals a *'cheer.'*

As a re-enactor the Rebel troops charge in with a cheer, but the same cheer as their adversaries, or some silly made up Hollywood type of idea, but there was a difference between the *'Union Cheer'* and the *'Rebel Yell'*. It was said that the *'Yell'* was a *'ki-yi'*, *'yip-yip-yip'*, *'woh-who-ey'*, *'wildcat screech'*, and a *'banshee squall'*.

The *' Yell'* would start at one end of the Confederate army and would sweep along to the other. Then it would sweep in waves up and down the line. However you shout it or describe it was the sound of the Southern Armies on the attack, and is the background sound on this page:
"They staggered, but closed up, and with the familiar "Hi-yi!" returned our fire and pressed forward with the savage courage of baited bulls." Gettysburg 1963.
"I heard heavy firing and the rebels 'Yelling' in the direction of the head of Hunting Run and surmised at once it was an attack on the right of the Eleventh Corps." Chancellorsville 1863.
"Our spirited fire, the sight of re-enforcements, and a terrific 'Rebel Yell' combined to strike terror to the foe, and he fled in confusion." Chattanooga 1863.
"About 4 o'clock the enemy charged our lines with such impetuosity that he quickly drove our infantry from the woods. With the peculiar 'Rebel Yell' they came on." Mine Run 1864.
"Soon the familiar 'Rebel Yell' broke upon the ear, and "see, they come," was the expression of all." North Anna River 1864.
"The first rebel line of battle emerged from the woods and came across the open field. This line was followed by two others, and with the true 'Rebel Yell' they came upon us."

Colonel Charles Dahnmon Whitt

Peach Tree Creek 1864.
The *" 'Rebel yell' burst out from the whole line, as all together they dashed at double quick toward the enemy."* Texans charging.

It was used at other times as well; during Thomas *'Stonewall'* Jackson's Valley Campaign, while in camp, one of the five regiments of the *'Stonewall'* Brigade began *'Yelling'*. Soon another regiment took it up and this carried on until every member of the entire Brigade doing the *'Yelling'*, so you can be sure that if one Brigade did something others would as well; other times were on the march with one regiment starting the *'Yell'* and it would then carry on down the road with all the others following joining in; it's also said that units would often wake up with the *'Yell'*.

It has been said that the *'Rebel Yell'* has been lost to us but a recording of a newsreel from the 1930's showing the reunion meeting marking the 75th Anniversary of the Battle of Gettysburg during the obligatory handshake one of the of old Confederate troops suddenly breaks into the *'Rebel Yell'*. This meeting, and the *'Yell'* are to be found on some of the reunion videos that are commercially available, it is also heard on Ken Burn's, *'The Civil War.'*

There is also in existence two recordings of Thomas N Alexander, 37th North Carolina Infantry, who at his first battle at 1st Cold Harbor (Gaines Mill), 1862, heard it. These are dated 1929 and 1932 respectively. One was in the studio of W.B.T. Radio and the other at a *'Sons of Confederate Veterans'* meeting. One is a group of veterans, W.B. Kidd, age 84; T.N. Alexander, age 92; D.W. Mayes, age 91; H.C. Irwin, age 90; J.E. Porter, age 96. The other is just by T.N. Alexander.

Confederate American

Another recording is supposedly in the possession of the *'United Daughters of the Confederacy'* and consists of a wax recording that is held at their national headquarters in Richmond, Virginia. This is recorded on a wax cylinder but there's some debate over whether it was recorded at a Florida *'U.D.C.'* Convention, just before the end of the 19th Century, or during the 1930s. It has been acknowledged by them that they do have this recording.

Written by an unknown Confederate after the Battle of the Wilderness *"At first (the Rebel Yell) heard like the rumbling of a distant train. It came rushing down the lines like the surging waves upon the ocean, increasing in loudness and grandeur, and passing, it could be heard dying on the left in the distance. Again it was heard coming from the right to die away again on the distant left. It was renewed three times, each with renewed vigor. It was a yell like the defiant tones of a thunderstorm."*

Henry E Tremain, (a Federal soldier on Major General Crook's staff) recalled they attacked *"With their peculiar faint cheer.*

John K. Bucklyn, (a Federal Artilleryman) used almost the same words *"With the peculiar rebel yell they came on."*

Gilbert Adams Hays (a Federal soldier) had this to *say "The peculiarity of the rebel yell is worthy of mention, but none of the old soldiers who heard it once will ever forget it. Instead of the deep-cheated manly cheer of the Union men, the rebel yell was a falsetto yelp which, when heard at a distance, reminded one of a lot of school boys at play. It was a peculiar affair for a battle yell, but though*

Colonel Charles Dahnmon Whitt

we made fun of it at first, we grew to respect it before the war is over. The yell might sound effeminate, but those who uttered it were not effeminate by any means. When the Union men charged, it was heads erect, shoulders squared and thrown back, and with a firm stride, but when the Johnnies charged, it was with a jog trot in a half bent position, and though they might be met with heavy and blighting volleys, they came on with the pertinacity of bulldogs, filling up gaps and trotting on with their never-ceasing "ki-yi" until we found them face to face."

Ambrose Bierce (a Federal soldier/author) wrote *"It was the ugliest sound any mortal ever heard."*

Arthur Freemantle (an English officer) said *"The Southern troops, when charging, or to express their delight, always yell in a manner peculiar to them. The Yankee cheer is much more like ours; but the Confederate officers declare that the Rebel yell has a particular merit, and always produces a salutary and useful effect upon their adversaries. A Corps is sometimes spoken of as a "good yelling regiment.""*

Warren Lee Goss (a Federal soldier) informs us that *"They charged upon us with their peculiar yell."*

James Harvie Dew, (a Confederate cavalryman with J.E.B. Stuart) He described the rebel yell *"In an instant every voice with one accord vigorously shouted the Rebel yell, which was so often heard on the field of battle...Woh--who--ey! Who--ey! Who--ey! Woh--who--ey! Who--ey!""*

Samuel Bradbury (a Federal engineer) on charging Rebels said *"And the Rebs a yelling as they came up on the charge with that peculiar yell they have. It sounds like a lot of school boys just let loose."*

Confederate American

George T Stevens (Federal soldier) talks of *"The vigorous manly cheers of the Northern soldiers, so different from the shrill yell of the Rebels."*

Newton Kirk (a Federal soldier) *"The shrill yells of the Rebels, mingled with the hoarser cheers of our own men."*

A doctor of the 4th New York remembered that *"Suddenly out of the dusk in front, and to the rear of us, burst the Ki-yi Ki-yi close to us and with it the Rebels were seen."*

Sidney Lanier (a Confederate soldier/poet) described it as *"A single long cry as from the leader of a pack of hounds.... a dry harsh quality that conveys an uncompromising hostility....a howl, a hoarse battle-cry, a cheer, and a congratulation, all in one."*

Keller Anderson of Kentucky's *'Orphan'* Brigade *"Then arose that do-or-die expression, that maniacal maelstrom of sound; that penetrating, rasping, shrieking, blood-curling noise that could be heard for miles..."*

New Orleans *'Times Picayune'* reporter *"It paragons description, that yell! How it starts deep and ends high, how it rises into three increasing crescendos and breaks with a command of battle."*

Thomas *'Stonewall'* Jackson (a Confederate General) thought it *"The sweetest music I ever heard."*

Jubal *'Old Jube'* Early (another Confederate General) said it *"is never mistaken for the studied hurrahs of the Yankees...."*

Colonel Charles Dahnmon Whitt

One Pennsylvanian infantryman remarked that *"when they got close enough they screamed that woman like scream and with fixed bayonet on they came."*

A Federal infantryman in Nelson A Mile's Division talks of *"The wild weird yells, which have become so familiar to our ears.'*

At Hatcher's Run a Federal newspaperman reported it saying they charged *"with the invariable yei, yei, yei of the Rebel (yell)."*

Other than the re-known *'Rebel Yell'* there was a soldier in the 26th Georgia, James Ervin Spivey, who was famed in both the Army of Northern Virginia and the Army of the Potomac for his battle cry. *"It was a kind of scream or low, like a terrible bull, with a kind of neigh mixed along with it, and it was nearly as loud as a steam whistle."* He was known as the *'Georgia Bull'*, by his comrades, and *'Gordon's Bull'*, by the Federals.

Late in the afternoon, at the Battle of Champions Hill, Sergeant William Ruyle reports *'They soon gave way in wild disorder. We gave the Missouri Yell and took after them.'* Assumedly just another name for the *'Rebel Yell.'*

There is a book published in 1954, *'The Blazing Southwest'* by Paul I Wellman, which claims that the *'Rebel Yell'* was originally used in the *'Texas War of Independence'* and was introduce into the Confederate Army by the Texan troops. The book has a quotation to support this, writer unnamed, *"it started with a low bass rumble and rose in a crescendo to a frenzied treble shriek which suggested a sort of berserk mania of blood lust."* This is different from the quotations above, written by those neither at the time, nor with the sound bite from the

Confederate American

newsreel that has come down to us.

Douglass Southall Freeman stated *"The rebel yell is pure legend. In Richmond it goes one way. In Atlanta you'll hear another. In Birmingham still another."* So it's quite possible that different units and armies gave different versions of the *'Yell'*, this would solve its different descriptions. It's nothing after all for soldiers to shout when in battle so *'yelling's'* nothing new it's been going on for time immemorial.

Where did the *'Rebel Yell'* come, from well many ideas have been suggested but as yet nothing is proven? Freeman thought it was an adaptation of the fox-hunters cry; a Virginian veteran that it came from a rural background when people had to shout out to each other in isolated areas

Source: Jim Brown (aka Gazkhan)

Colonel Charles Dahnmon Whitt

Chapter 15
Flags of the Confederates

Here's a little history about our Georgia State flag as it should still be flying, I will never accept the new "Flag of Atlanta". I believe that the Confederate flag stands for anything, but hate and contempt. It stands for much, much more, our freedom to be Southern and to be proud of our ancestors and our heritage. So I say "Let It Fly", always a symbol of the "Proud South".

The Flag on the left is the Confederate National Flag and the Right is the Battle Flag. The Battle Flag is red with the bars being blue and the stars being white.

After the election of Abraham Lincoln as President in November of 1860, unofficial flags consisting of a single

Confederate American

star on a solid background began appearing across the South. As each star on the U.S. flag signified a state, a single star indicated that the state had withdrawn (or planned to withdraw) from the Union, which would make it a sovereign power.

Among the early actions was appointment of a committee to propose a new flag and seal for the Confederacy. The proposal adopted by the commission called for a flag consisting of a red field divided by a white band one-third the width of the field, making three bars of equal width. The flag had a blue square the height of two bars, on which was placed a circle of white stars corresponding in number to the States of the Confederacy. South Carolina, Mississippi, Florida, Alabama, Georgia, Louisiana, and Texas. It soon came to be known as the *"Stars and Bars"*. With 7 stars at first, the number jumped to 11 with the secession of Virginia, Arkansas, North Carolina and Tennessee, and finally 13 (in recognition of the symbolic admission of Kentucky and Missouri to the Confederacy).

CONFEDERATE BATTLE FLAG 1861 - 1865

Red background, blue cross bars with white stars.

Colonel Charles Dahnmon Whitt

Confederate General P.G.T. Beauregard and Joseph Johnston urged that a new Confederate flag be designed for battle. The result was the square flag sometimes known as the "Southern Cross" The Confederate Battle Flag consisted of a blue satire, resembling the Saint Andrew's cross, on which were 13 stars, with the satire edged in white, all on a red background.

2nd NATIONAL FLAG of the CONFEDERACY 1863 - 1865

Second Confederate Battle Flag in corner on white banner. They changed this flag as it was confused as a Flag of Surrender!

Throughout the spring of 1863, the Confederate Congress debated the design for a new National flag. On May 1, the last day of the session both houses agreed to a flag consisting of a white field. It was widely known as the "Stainless Banner". Because the 1st issue of this flag was draped on the coffin of General Thomas J. "Stonewall" Jackson, it was also known as the "Jackson Flag".

3rd NATIONAL FLAG of the CONFEDERACY, 1865

Third Confederate This third National flag had a wide strip of red on the end. This was no flag of surrender.

Although The War for Southern Independence was in its final stages, President Jefferson Davis signed legislation on March 4, 1865, creating the 3rd National flag of the Confederacy. The new banner had a width two-thirds of its length. The flag's "Confederate Battle Flag" changed

Confederate American

from a square to a rectangle three-fifths the width of the flag itself and of a length so that the field beyond it measured twice the width of the field below it. The flag continued to use a white field to the right of the Battle Flag canton consisted of a red band. Authorized in the final months of the war, relatively few copies of the 3rd National flag were made and even fewer survived.

GEORGIA STATE FLAG before 1879 (unofficial)

 the three wide stripes are two red and one blue. The stars are white on blue background.

History does not record who made the first Georgia State flag, when it was made, what it looked like, or who authorized its creation. In 1861, a new provision was added to Georgia's code requiring the governor to supply regimental flags to Georgia militia units assigned to fight outside the state. These flags were to depict the "arms of the state" and the name of the regiment, but the code gave no indication as to the color to be used on the arms, which is the prominent design-usually shown on a shield-located at the center of an armorial bearing or seal.

GEORGIA STATE FLAG 1879 - 1902

In 1879, state senator Herman H. Perry introduced legislation giving Georgia its first official state flag. The

Colonel Charles Dahnmon Whitt

legislation provided no height vs. length dimensions, but it did state that the width of the blue band be one-third the length of the flag. Also, the red of the flag was specified to be Scarlet. Governor Colquitt approved Georgia's first official state flag on October 17, 1879.

GEORGIA STATE FLAG, c.1902 - 1906

In 1902, as part of another major reorganization of state military laws, the General Assembly changed Georgia's state flag again. A new addition stated that "On the blue field shall be stamped, painted or embroidered the coat of arms of the State; and every regiment and unassigned battalion shall, when on parade, carry this flag."

GEORGIA STATE FLAG, c. 1906 - 1920

Between 1902 and 1906, some unknown person or flag manufacturer added a gold-outlined white shield to the coat of arms, placed a date "1799" below the arms, and

Confederate American

added a red ribbon with "Georgia" below the shield. Although the General Assembly had not authorized any changes to the state flag, apparently no one contested the new version.

GEORGIA STATE FLAG, c. 1920 - 1956

By the late 1910's or early 1920's, a new, unofficial version of Georgia's state flag -- one incorporating the entire state seal -- began appearing. The new flag may have resulted from a 1914 law changing the date on Georgia's state seal from 1799 (the date the seal was adopted) to 1776 (the year of independence).

GEORGIA STATE FLAG SINCE 1956

In early 1955, Atlanta attorney John Sammons Bell (who later served as a judge on the Georgia Court of Appeals) suggested a new state flag for Georgia that would incorporate the Confederate Battle Flag. At the 1956 session of the General Assembly, state senators Jefferson Lee Davis (Not the President of the Confederacy.) and Willis Harden introduced Senate Bill 98 to change the state flag. Signed into law on February 13, 1956, the bill became effective the following July 1.
In the 1956 version, the stars are larger, and only the

Colonel Charles Dahnmon Whitt

center point of the central star points up. Also the first copies of the 1956 flag used a different version of the state seal.

From 1861 until 1865 there were two quite different views of Old Glory. U.S. Flag was all but worshipped in the North; it was hated *in the South. Now almost the opposite is true about the Confederate Flag.*

Bonny Blue Flag, (Blue with a single white star.) It was raised over Charleston in 1861 as a symbol of strength and "We are a band of brothers."

Blue flag with one big white star.
From Wikipedia, the free encyclopedia

    "**The Bonnie Blue Flag**", also known as "**We Are a Band of Brothers**", is an 1861 marching song associated with the Confederate States of America. The words were written by Irish born entertainer Harry McCarthy, with the melody taken from the song "The Irish Jaunting Car". The song's title refers to the unofficial first Flag of the Confederacy, the "Bonnie Blue Flag, the symbol of secession from the Union, which bears the "single star" of the chorus.

"The Bonnie Blue Flag" holds special significance to the Texas brigade. The song was premiered by lyricist Harry McCarthy during a concert in Jackson, Mississippi, in the

Confederate American

spring of 1861 and performed again in September of that same year at the New Orleans Academy of Music for the First Texas Volunteer Infantry regiment mustering in celebration.

Source: Wikipedia, the free encyclopedia

Flag carried by Infantry Units defending the Commonwealth of Virginia. They also carried the Confederate National flags.

Though flags similar to Virginia's current flag had flown in the State since the 1830s, Virginia did not adopt an official flag until after it had seceded from the Union in 1861. The Flag of the Commonwealth was adopted on April 30, 1861 almost two weeks after Virginia voted, on April 17, 1861, to repeal its 1788 ratification of the Constitution of the United

Colonel Charles Dahnmon Whitt

States. The Virginia Flag of the Commonwealth displays the State Seal of Virginia centered on a blue field (background).

From January through mid-April, delegates to the 1861 Virginia Convention staved off efforts to vote Virginia out of the Union but their efforts fell short on April 17, perhaps assisted by the announcement that President Abraham Lincoln had just called for 75,000 volunteers for the Union army. In a vote adopting "An Ordinance to repeal the ratification of the Constitution of the United States of America, by the State of Virginia, and to resume all the rights and powers granted under said Constitution," Virginia declared its sovereignty and opened the way for the Commonwealth to join the Confederate States of America (CSA).

On April 30, 1861, a flag very similar to the current flag was adopted when Ordinance No. 30 was embraced by the Virginia Convention of 1861 -- The Secession Convention. This ordinance was ratified by a vote of the electorate in May.

No. 33 -- An ORDINANCE to establish a Flag for this Commonwealth

Be it ordained by the convention of the commonwealth of Virginia, that the flag of this commonwealth shall hereafter be made of bunting, which shall be a deep blue field with a circle of white in the center, upon which shall be painted or embroidered, to show on both sides alike, the coat of arms of the state, as described by the convention of

Confederate American

seventeen hundred and seventy-six, for one side of the seal of state, to wit:

"Virtus, the genius of the commonwealth, dressed like an Amazon, resting on a spear with one hand, and holding a sword in other, and treading on tyranny, represented by a man prostrate, a crown fallen from his head, a broken chain in his left hand and a scourge in his right. In the exergon the word Virginia over the head of Virtus, and underneath the words "Sic Semper Tyrannis."

This flag shall be known and respected as the flag of Virginia.

The governor shall regulate the size and dimensions of the flag proper for forts, arsenals and public buildings, for ships of war and merchant marine, for troops in the field, respectively, and for any other purpose, according to his discretion; which regulations shall be published and proclaimed by him as occasion may require.

This ordinance shall take effect from its passage.

Virginia joined the Confederates States of America in 1861, after they learned that Abraham Lincoln called for a Northern army of 75,000 to be raised to make the southern states stay in the union.

During the Civil War, Virginia regiments flew the newly adopted Flag, of the Commonwealth along with the two national flags of the Confederate States of America.

Colonel Charles Dahnmon Whitt
Chapter 16
Songs of the Confederates

ALL QUIET ALONG THE POTOMAC

By Ethel Lynn Eliot Beers

"All quiet along the Potomac to-night!"
   Except here and there a stray picket
Is shot, as he walks on his beat, to and fro,
   By a rifleman hid in the thicket.
'Tis nothing! a private or two now and then
   Will not count in the news of a battle;
Not an officer lost, only one of the men
   Moaning out, all alone, the death rattle.

All quiet along the Potomac to-night!
   Where the soldiers lie peacefully dreaming;
And their tents in the rays of the clear autumn moon,
   And the light of their camp-fires are gleaming.
A tremulous sigh, as a gentle night-wind
   Through the forest leaves slowly is creeping;
While the stars up above, with their glittering eyes,
   Keep guard o'er the army sleeping.
There's only the sound of the lone sentry's tread
   As he tramps from the rock to the fountain,
And thinks of the two on the low trundle bed,
   Far away, in the cot on the mountain.

His musket falls slack, his face, dark and grim,
   Grows gentle with memories tender,
As he mutters a prayer for the children asleep,

Confederate American

And their mother--"may heaven defend her!"
The moon seems to shine forth as brightly as then--
   That night, when the love, yet unspoken,
Leaped up to his lips, and when low-murmured vows
   Were pledged to be ever unbroken.

Then drawing his sleeve roughly over his eyes,
   He dashes off tears that are welling;
And gathers the gun closer up to his breast
   As if to keep down his heart's swelling.
He passes the fountain, the blasted pine-tree,
   And his footstep is lagging and weary;
Yet onward he goes, through the broad belt of light,
   Towards the shades of the forest so dreary.

Hark! was it the night-wind that rustled the leaves?
   Was it the moonlight so wondrously flashing?
It looked like a rifle: "Ha! Mary, good-by!"
   And his life-blood is ebbing and plashing.
"All quiet along the Potomac to-night!"
   No sound save the rush of the river;
While soft falls the dew on the face of the dead,
   And the picket's off duty forever!

THE BATTLE CRY OF FREEDOM

Music by George F. Root

(1820-1895)

Our flag is proudly floating
  On the land and on the main,

Colonel Charles Dahnmon Whitt

Shout, shout the battle cry of Freedom!
  Beneath it oft we've conquered,
And we'll conquer oft again!
  Shout, shout the battle cry of Freedom!

CHORUS: Our Dixie forever!
  She's never at a loss!
Down with the eagle
  And up with the cross!
We'll rally 'round the bonny flag,
  We'll rally once again,
Shout, shout the battle cry of Freedom!

Our gallant boys have marched
  To the rolling of the drums,
Shout, shout the battle cry of Freedom!
  And the leaders in charge cry out,
"Come, boys, come!"
  Shout, shout the battle cry of Freedom!--**CHORUS**

They have laid down their lives
  On the bloody battle field,
Shout, shout the battle cry of Freedom!
  Their motto is resistance --
"To tyrants we'll not yield!"
  Shout, shout the battle cry of Freedom!--**CHORUS**

While our boys have responded
  And to the fields have gone,
Shout, shout the battle cry of Freedom!
Our noble women also
  Have aided them at home,
Shout, shout the battle cry of Freedom!—

Confederate American

THE BONNIE BLUE FLAG

Lyrics by Harry Macarthy (d. 1880)

We are a band of brothers
   And native to the soil,
Fighting for the property
   We gained by honest toil;
And when our rights were threatened,
   The cry rose near and far--
"Hurrah for the Bonnie Blue Flag
   That bears a single star!"

CHORUS: Hurrah! Hurrah!
   For Southern rights hurrah!
Hurrah for the Bonnie Blue Flag
   That bears a single star.

As long as the Union
   Was faithful to her trust,
Like friends and like brothers
   Both kind were we and just;
But now, when Northern treachery
   Attempts our rights to mar,
We hoist on high the Bonnie Blue Flag
   That bears a single star.--**CHORUS**

First gallant South Carolina
   Nobly made the stand,
Then came Alabama,
   Who took her by the hand?
Next quickly Mississippi,
   Georgia and Florida
All raised on high the Bonnie Blue Flag

Colonel Charles Dahnmon Whitt

  That bears a single star.--**CHORUS**

Ye men of valor, gather round
  The banner of the right;
Texas and fair Louisiana
  Join us in the fight.
Davis, our loved president,
  And Stephens statesman are;
Now rally round the Bonnie Blue Flag
  That bears a single star.--**CHORUS**

And here's to old Virginia--
  The Old Dominion State--
Who with the young Confederacy
  At length has linked her fate;
Impelled by her example,
  Now other states prepare
To hoist on high the Bonnie Blue Flag
  That bears a single star.--**CHORUS**

Then cheer, boys, cheer;
  Raise the joyous shout,
For Arkansas and North Carolina
  Now have both gone out;
And let another rousing cheer
  For Tennessee be given,
The single star of the Bonnie Blue Flag
  Has grown to be eleven.--**CHORUS**

Then here's to our Confederacy,
  Strong are we and brave;
Like patriots of old we'll fight
  Our heritage to save.
And rather than submit to shame,
  To die we would prefer;
So cheer for the Bonnie Blue Flag

Confederate American

That bears a single star.--**CHORUS**

CHEER, BOYS, CHEER!

Lyricist Unknown

CHORUS: Cheer, boys, cheer! We'll march away to battle!
Cheer, boys, cheer, for our sweethearts and our wives!
Cheer, boys, cheer! We'll nobly do our duty,
And give to the South our hearts, our arms, our lives.

Bring forth the flag, our country's noble standard;
Wave it on high till the wind shakes each fold out.
Proudly it floats, nobly waving in the vanguard;
Then cheer, boys, cheer! with a lusty, long, bold shout.

CHORUS

But as we march, with heads all lowly bending,
Let us implore a blessing from on high.
Our cause is just, the right we're defending,
And the God of battle will listen to our cry.

CHORUS

Tho' to the homes we never may return,
Ne'er press again our lov'd ones in our arms,
O'er our lone graves their faithful hearts will mourn,
Then cheer, boys, cheer! such death hath no alarms.

Colonel Charles Dahnmon Whitt
DIXIE'S LAND

by Daniel Decatur Emmett

(1815-1904)

I wish I was in the land of cotton,
Old times there are not forgotten;
   Look away! Look away! Look away, Dixie's Land!
In Dixie's Land where I was born in,
Early on one frosty morning,
   Look away! Look away! Look away, Dixie's Land!

CHORUS: Then I wish I was in Dixie! Hooray! Hooray!
In Dixie's Land I'll take my stand, to live and die in Dixie!
Away! Away! Away down South in Dixie!
Away! Away! Away down South in Dixie!

Old Missus married "Will the Weaver";
William was a gay deceiver!
   Look away! Look away! Look away, Dixie's Land!
But when he put his arm around her,
Smiled as fierce as a forty-pounder!
   Look away! Look away! Look away, Dixie's Land!--
CHORUS

His face was sharp as a butcher's cleaver;
But that did not seem to grieve her!
   Look away! Look away! Look away, Dixie's Land!
Old Missus acted the foolish part
And died for a man that broke her heart!
   Look away! Look away! Look away, Dixie's Land!--
CHORUS

Now here's a health to the next old missus
And all the gals that want to kiss us!

Confederate American

    Look away! Look away! Look away, Dixie's Land!
But if you want to drive away sorrow,
Come and hear this song tomorrow!
    Look away! Look away! Look away, Dixie's Land!--
CHORUS

There's buckwheat cakes and Injin batter,
Makes you fat or a little fatter!
    Look away! Look away! Look away, Dixie's Land!
Then hoe it down and scratch your gravel,
To Dixie's Land I'm bound to travel!
    Look away! Look away! Look away, Dixie's Land!--
CHORUS

GOD SAVE THE SOUTH

Words by Earnest Halpin

Music by Charles W.A. Ellerbrock

God save the South, God save the South,
Her altars and firesides, God save the South!
Now that the war is nigh, now that we arm to die,
Chanting our battle cry, "Freedom or death!"
Chanting our battle cry, "Freedom or death!"

God be our shield, at home or afield,
Stretch Thine arm over us, strengthen and save.
What tho' they're three to one, forward each sire and son,
Strike till the war is won, strike to the grave!
Strike till the war is won, strike to the grave!

Colonel Charles Dahnmon Whitt

God made the right stronger than might,
Millions would trample us down in their pride.
Lay Thou their legions low, roll back the ruthless foe,
Let the proud spoiler know God's on our side.
Let the proud spoiler know God's on our side.

Hark honor's call, summoning all.
Summoning all of us unto the strife.
Sons of the South, awake! Strike till the brand shall break,
Strike for dear Honor's sake, Freedom and Life!
Strike for dear Honor's sake, Freedom and Life!

Rebels before, our fathers of yore.
Rebel's the righteous name Washington bore.
Why, then, be ours the same, the name that he snatched from shame,
Making it first in fame, foremost in war.
Making it first in fame, foremost in war.

War to the hilt, theirs be the guilt,
Who fetter the free man to ransom the slave.
Up then, and undismay'd, sheathe not the battle blade,
Till the last foe is laid low in the grave!
Till the last foe is laid low in the grave!

God save the South, God save the South,
Dry the dim eyes that now follow our path.
Still let the light feet rove safe through the orange grove,
Still keep the land we love safe from Thy wrath.
Still keep the land we love safe from Thy wrath.

God save the South, God save the South,
Her altars and firesides, God save the South!
For the great war is nigh, and we will win or die,
Chanting our battle cry, "Freedom or death!"
Chanting our battle cry, "Freedom or death!"

Confederate American

GOOBER PEAS

by A. Pindar

Sittin' by the roadside on a summer's day,
Chattin' with my messmates, passing time away,
Lying in the shadows, underneath the trees --
Goodness, how delicious, eating goober peas!

CHORUS: Peas! Peas! Peas! Peas! Eating goober peas!
Goodness, how delicious, eating goober peas!

When a horseman passes, the soldiers have a rule
To cry out at their loudest "Mister, here's your mule!"
But still another pleasure enchantinger than these
Is wearing out your grinders, eating goober peas!

CHORUS

Just before the battle, the General hears a row;
He says "The Yanks are coming, I hear their rifles now"!
He turns around in wonder, and what do you think he sees?
The Georgia Militia, eating goober peas!

CHORUS

I think my song had lasted almost long enough!
The subject's interesting, but rhymes are mighty rough!
I wish this war was over, when free from rags and fleas,

Colonel Charles Dahnmon Whitt

We'd kiss our wives and sweethearts and goble goober peas! Goober Peas are Peanuts, for my Yankee friends.)

THE HOMESPUN DRESS

by Carrie Belle Sinclair

(Born 1839)

Oh, yes, I am a Southern girl,
   And glory in the name,
And boast it with far greater pride
   Than glittering wealth and fame.
We envy not the Northern girl
   Her robes of beauty rare,
Though diamonds grace her snowy neck
   And pearls bedeck her hair.

CHORUS: Hurrah! Hurrah!
   For the sunny South so dear;
Three cheers for the homespun dress
   The Southern ladies wear!

The homespun dress is plain, I know,
   My hat's palmetto, too;
But then it shows what Southern girls
   For Southern rights will do.
We send the bravest of our land
   To battle with the foe,
And we will lend a helping hand--
   We love the South, you know.--**CHORUS**

Now Northern goods are out of date;
   And since old Abe's blockade,
We Southern girls can be content

Confederate American

   With goods that's Southern made.
We send our sweethearts to the war;
   But, dear girls, never mind--
Your soldier-love will ne'er forget
   The girl he left behind.--**CHORUS**

The soldier is the lad for me--
   A brave heart I adore;
And when the sunny South is free,
   And when fighting is no more,
I'll choose me then a lover brave
   From all that gallant band;
The soldier lad I love the best
   Shall have my heart and hand.--**CHORUS**

The Southern land's a glorious land,
   And has a glorious cause;
Then cheer, three cheers for Southern rights,
   And for the Southern boys!
We scorn to wear a bit of silk,
   A bit of Northern lace,
But make our homespun dresses up,
   And wear them with a grace.--**CHORUS**

And now, young man, a word to you:
   If you would win the fair,
Go to the field where honor calls,
   And win your lady there.
Remember that our brightest smiles
   Are for the true and brave,
And that our tears are all for those
   Who fill a soldier's grave?

Colonel Charles Dahnmon Whitt

PICKING LINT

J. W. Barker

Plying the busy fingers
Over the vestments old,
Not with the weary needle,
Not for some grains of gold;
Thinking of fainting heroes,
Out in the dreary night,
Smitten in Freedom's battle,
First in the gallant fight --

CHORUS:
O, bright are the jewels from love's deep mint,
God bless the fingers while picking the lint,
God bless the fingers while picking the lint.

Quicker, the blood is flowing,
Hundreds were slain today,
And every warm pulsation
Is stealing life away.
"A hundred threads a minute,
A hundred drops of gore,"
The sad and thrilling measures
We've never learned before --

CHORUS:
The shadows are weaving a silver tint,
God bless the fingers while picking the lint,
God bless the fingers while picking the lint.

We've clad the fallen heroes
With garments we have made,

Confederate American

By light we now are picking,
The fearful tide be stayed;
We lift our hearts to Heaven,
Our Father's blessings crave,
Behold our smitten country,
O bless the fallen brave --

CHORUS:
O, bright are the jewels from love's deep mint,
God bless the fingers while picking the lint,
God bless the fingers while picking the lint.

YOU ARE GOING TO THE WARS, WILLie BOY!

By John Hill Hewitt

You are going to the wars, Willie boy, Willie boy,
You are going to the wars far away,
To protect our rights and laws, Willie boy, Willie boy,
And the banner in the sun's golden ray;
With your uniform all new,
And you're shining buttons too,
You'll win the hearts of pretty girls,
But none like me so true.
Oh! Won't you think of me, Willie boy, Willie boy;
Oh, won't you think of me when far away?
I'll often think of you, Willie boy, Willie boy,
And ever for your life and glory pray.

You'll be fighting for the right, Willie boy, Willie boy,
You'll be fighting for the right and your home;
And you'll strike the blow with might, Willie boy, Willie boy,

Colonel Charles Dahnmon Whitt

'Mid the thundering of cannon and drum;
With an arm as true as steel,
You'll make the foeman feel
The vengeance of a Southerner
Too pride to cringe or kneel.
Oh! should you fall in strife, Willie boy, Willie boy;
Oh, should you fall in strife on the plain,
I'll pine away my life, Willie boy, Willie boy,
And never, never wear a smile again.

THE YELLOW ROSE OF TEXAS

There's a yellow rose in Texas
  That I am going to see.
No other soldier knows her --
  No soldier, only me.
She cried so when I left her,
  It like to broke my heart,
And if I ever find her,
  We never more shall part.

CHORUS: She's the sweetest rose of color
  This soldier ever knew.
Her eyes are bright as diamonds,
  They sparkle like the dew.
You may talk about your dearest May
  And sing of Rosa Lee,
But the Yellow Rose of Texas
  Beats the belles of Tennessee.

Where the Rio Grande is flowing
  And the starry skies are bright,
She walks along the river

Confederate American

In the quiet summer night.
She thinks, if I remember,
  When we parted long ago,
I promised to come back again
  And not to leave her so.--**CHORUS**

Oh, now I'm going to find her,
  For my heart is full of woe,
And we'll sing the song together
  That we sang so long ago.
We'll play the banjo gaily,
  And we'll sing the songs of yore,
And the Yellow Rose of Texas
  Shall be mine forever more.--**CHORUS**

Oh, now I'm headed southward,
  For my heart is full of woe.
I'm going back to Georgia
  To find my Uncle Joe.
You may talk about your Beauregard
  And sing of Bobby Lee,
But the gallant Hood of Texas,
  He played hell in Tennessee! **CHORUS**

WHEN JOHNNY COMES MARCHING HOME

by Patrick Sarsfield Gilmore

When Johnny comes marching home again,
Hurrah! Hurrah!
We'll give him a hearty welcome then,
Hurrah! Hurrah!

Colonel Charles Dahnmon Whitt

The men will cheer, the boys will shout,
The ladies they will all turn out,
And we'll all feel gay
When Johnny comes marching home.

The old church bells will peal with joy,
Hurrah! Hurrah!
To welcome home our darling boy,
Hurrah! Hurrah!
The village lads and lassies say
With roses they will strew the way,
And we'll all feel gay
When Johnny comes marching home.

Get ready for the Jubilee,
Hurrah! Hurrah!
We'll give the hero three times three,
Hurrah! Hurrah!
The laurel wreath is ready now
To place upon his loyal brow,
And we'll all feel gay
When Johnny comes marching home.

Let love and friendship on that day,
Hurrah! Hurrah!
Their choicest treasures then display,
Hurrah! Hurrah!
And let each one perform some part
To fill with joy the warrior's heart,
And we'll all feel gay
When Johnny comes marching home.

Confederate American

STONEWALL JACKSON'S WAY

By John Williamson Palmer

(1825-1906)

Come, stack arms, men. Pile on the rails,
   Stir up the campfire bright;
No matter if the canteen fails,
   We'll make a roaring night.
Here Shenandoah brawls along,
   There burly Blue Ridge echoes strong
To swell the brigade's rousing song
   Of "Stonewall Jackson's way."

We see him now--the old slouched hat
   Cocked o'er his eye askew--
The shrewd, dry smile--the speech so pat--
   So calm, so blunt, so true.
That "Blue-Light Elder" knows 'em well--
   Says he, "That's Banks; he's fond of shell--
Lord save his soul! We'll give him"...well,
   That's "Stonewall Jackson's way."

Silence! Ground arms! kneel all! caps off!
   Old Blue Light's going to pray;
Strangle the fool that dares to scoff;
   Attention; it's his way!
Appealing from his native sod,
   In forma pauperis to God--
"Lay bare thine arm; stretch forth thy rod;
Amen." That's "Stonewall's way."

Colonel Charles Dahnmon Whitt

He's in the saddle now! Fall in!
   Steady, the whole brigade!
Hill's at the ford, cut off! He'll win
   His way out, ball and blade.
What matter if our shoes are worn?
   What matter if our feet are torn?
"Quick step--we're with him ere the dawn!"
   That's "Stonewall Jackson's way."

The sun's bright glances rout the mists
   Of morning, and, by George!
There's Longstreet struggling in the lists,
   Hemmed in an ugly gorge--
Pope and his Yankees whipped before--
   "Bayonet and grape!" hear Stonewall roar,
"Charge, Stuart! Pay off Ashby's score
   In Stonewall Jackson's way."

Ah, maiden! wait and watch and yearn
   For news of Stonewall's band!
Ah, widow! read with eyes that burn
   That ring upon thy hand!
Ah, wife! sew on, pray on, hope on,
   Thy life shall not be all forlorn--
The foe had better ne'er been born,
   That gets in Stonewall's way.

Confederate American

Thomas J. "Stonewall" Jackson
from "Lord of the Valley" by Dale Gallon

Colonel Charles Dahnmon Whitt

SOMEBODY'S DARLING

Words by Marie Ravenal de la Coste

Into the ward of the clean white-washed halls,
Where the dead slept and the dying lay;
Wounded by bayonets, sabres and balls,
Somebody's darling was borne one day.
Somebody's darling, so young and so brave,
Wearing still on his sweet yet pale face,
Soon to be hid in the dust of the grave,
The lingering light of his boyhood's grace.

CHORUS: Somebody's darling, somebody's pride,
Who'll tell his mother where her boy died?

Matted and damp are his tresses of gold,
Kissing the snow of that fair young brow;
Pale are the lips of most delicate mould,
Somebody's darling is dying now.
Back from his beautiful purple-veined brow,
Brush off the wandering waves of gold;
Cross his white hands on his broad bosom now,
Somebody's darling is still and cold.--**CHORUS**

Give him a kiss, but for somebody's sake,
Murmur a prayer for him, soft and low,
One little curl from his golden mates take,
Somebody's they were once, you know;
Somebody's warm hand has oft rested there,
Was it a Mother's so soft and white?
Or have the lips of a sister, so fair,
Ever been bathed in their waves of light? --**CHORUS**

Somebody's watching and waiting for him,

Confederate American

Yearning to hold him again to her breast;
Yet there he lies with his blue eyes so dim,
And purple, child-like lips half apart.
Tenderly bury the fair, unknown dead,
Pausing to drop on his grave a tear;
Carve on the wooden slab over his head,
"Somebody's darling is slumbering here."--**CHORUS**

MARYLAND, MY MARYLAND

By James Ryder Randall

(1839-1908)

The despot's heel is on thy shore,
Maryland, my Maryland!
His torch is at thy temple door,
Maryland, my Maryland!
Avenge the patriotic gore
That flecked the streets of Baltimore,
And be the battle queen of yore,
Maryland, my Maryland!

Hark to an exiled son's appeal,
Maryland, my Maryland!
My mother state, to thee I kneel,
Maryland, my Maryland!
For life or death, for woe or weal,
Thy peerless chivalry reveal,
And gird they beauteous limbs with steel,
Maryland, my Maryland!

Thou wilt not cower in the dust,
Maryland, my Maryland!
Thy beaming sword shall never rust,

Colonel Charles Dahnmon Whitt

Maryland, my Maryland!
Remember Caroll's sacred trust.
Remember Howard's warlike thrust,
And all thy slumberers with the just,
Maryland, my Maryland.

Come! 'Tis the red dawn of the day,
Maryland, my Maryland!
Come with thy panoplied array,
Maryland, my Maryland!
With Ringgold's spirit for the fray,
With Watson's blood at Monterey,
With fearless Lowe and dashing May,
Maryland, my Maryland!

Dear Mother, burst the tyrant's chain,
Maryland, my Maryland!
Virginia should not call in vain,
Maryland, my Maryland!
She meets her sisters on the plain,
"Sic semper!" 'Tis the proud refrain
That baffles minions back amain,
Maryland, my Maryland!
Arise in majesty again,
Maryland, my Maryland!

Come! For thy shield is brighter and strong,
Maryland, my Maryland!
Come! For thy dalliance does thee wrong,
Maryland, my Maryland!
Come to thine own heroic throng,
Stalking with Liberty along,
And chant thy dauntless slogan-song,
Maryland, my Maryland!

I see the blush upon thy cheek,

Confederate American

Maryland, my Maryland!
But thou wast ever bravely meek,
Maryland, my Maryland!
But lo! There surges forth a shriek,
From hill to hill, from creek to creek,
Potomac calls to Chesapeake,
Maryland, my Maryland!

Thou wilt not yield the vandal toll,
Maryland, my Maryland!
Thou wilt not crook to his control,
Maryland, my Maryland!
Better the fire upon the roll,
Better the shot, the blade, the bowl,
Than crucifixion of the soul,
Maryland, my Maryland.

I hear the distant thunder-hum,
Maryland, my Maryland!
The "old line's" bugle, fife and drum,
Maryland, my Maryland!
She is not dead, nor deaf, nor dumb;
Huzza! She spurns the Northern scum --
She breathes! She burns! She'll come! She'll come!
Maryland, my Maryland!

ROSE OF ALABAMY

Away from Mississippi's vale,
With my ol' hat there for a sail,
I crossed upon a cotton bale
To Rose of Alabamy.

Colonel Charles Dahnmon Whitt

CHORUS: Oh brown Rosie,
Rose of Alabamy!
A sweet tobacco posey
Is my Rose of Alabamy.

I landed on the far sand bank,
I sat upon the hollow plank,
And there I made the banjo twank
For Rose of Alabamy.--**CHORUS**

Oh, after d'rectly bye and bye,
The moon rose white as Rosie's eye;
Then like a young coon out so sly
Stole Rose of Alabamy.--**CHORUS**

I said "Sit down just where you please."
Upon my lap she took her ease.
"It's good to go upon the knees,"
Said Rose of Alabamy.--**CHORUS**

The river rose; the cricket sang,
The lightnin' bug did flash his wing;
Then like a rope my arms I fling,
'Round Rose of Alabamy.--**CHORUS**

We hugged how long I cannot tell.
My Rosie seemed to like it well.
My banjo in the river fell.
Oh, Rose of Alabamy.--**CHORUS**

Like alligator after prey,
I jump in, but it float away,
And all the while it seem to say,
"Oh, Rose of Alabamy."--**CHORUS**

Now every night come rain or shower,

Confederate American

I hunt that banjo for an hour;
And see my sweet tobacco flower,
Oh, Rose of Alabamy.--**CHORUS**

Oh fare thee well, you belles of Spain,
And fare thee well to Liza Jane!
Your charms will all be put to shame,
By Rose of Alabamy.--**CHORUS**

SOUTHERN SOLDIER BOY

Words: Captain G.W. Alexander

Tune: "The Boy with the Auburn Hair"

Bob Roebuck is my sweetheart's name,
He's off to the wars and gone;
He's fighting for his Nanny dear,
His sword is buckled on,
He's fighting for his own true love;
His foes he does defy;
He is the darling of my heart,
My Southern soldier boy.

When Bob comes home from war's alarms,
We'll start anew in life;
I'll give myself right up to him,
A dutiful, loving wife.
I'll try my best to please my dear,
For he is my only joy,

Colonel Charles Dahnmon Whitt

He is the darling of my heart,
My Southern soldier boy.

Oh, if in battle he were slain,
I know that I would die,
But I am sure he'll come again
To cheer my weeping eye.
But should he fall in this our glorious cause,
He still would be my joy,
For many a sweetheart mourns the loss
Of her Southern soldier boy.

I hope for the best, and so do all
Whose hopes are in the field;
I know that we shall win the day
For Southern's never yield.
And when we think of those who are away,
We look above for joy,
And I'm mighty glad that my Bobby is
A Southern soldier boy.

O, I'm a Good Old Rebel

NOTE: In the book Point Lookout Prison Camp for Confederates, Edwin Beitzell says, "*According to Herbert Quick, who printed an account of The Good Old Rebel in Colliers for April 14, 1914, its author was Major James Randolph, a Virginian and a member of General J.E.B. Stuart's staff. Sung to the tune of Joe Bowers, a favorite of the forty-niners, it traveled beyond the bounds of the Confederacy. Edward VII, the Prince of Wales, heard it at a reception in London and called it 'that fine American song with the cuss words in it.*"

Confederate American

O, I'm a good old Rebel,
Now that's just what I am,
For this "Fair Land of Freedom"
I do not care at all;

I'm glad I fit against it --
I only wish we'd won,
And I don't want no pardon
For anything I done.

I hates the Constitution,
This Great Republic too,
I hates the Freedman's Buro,
In uniforms of blue;

I hates the nasty eagle,
With all his brags and fuss,
The lyin', thievin' Yankees,
I hates 'em wuss and wuss.

I hates the Yankee nation
And everything they do,
I hates the Declaration
Of Independence too;

I hates the glorious Union --
'Tis dripping with our blood --
I hates their striped banner,
I fit it all I could.

Colonel Charles Dahnmon Whitt

I followed old mass' Robert
For four year, near about,
Got wounded in three places
And starved at Pint Lookout;

I cotch the rheumatism
A campin' in the snow,
But I killed a chance of Yankees,
I'd like to kill some mo'.

Three hundred thousand Yankees
Is stiff in Southern dust;
We got three hundred thousand
Before they conquered us;

They died of Southern fever
And Southern steel and shot,
I wish they was three million
Instead of what we got.

I can't take up my musket
And fight 'em now no more,
But I ain't going to love 'em,
Now that is sarten sure;

And I don't want no pardon
For what I was and am,
I won't be reconstructed
And I don't care a damn.

Confederate American
Chapter 17
Women as Weapons

Belle Boyd:
She passed information on Union army movements in the Shenandoah to General T. J. (Stonewall) Jackson, and was imprisoned as a spy. She wrote a book on her exploits.

Antonia Ford:
She informed General J.E.B. Stuart of Union activity near her Fairfax, Virginia, home. She married a Union major who helped gain her release.

Rose O'Neal Greenhow :
A popular society hostess in Washington, DC, she used her contacts to gain information to pass to the Confederacy. Imprisoned for a time for her espionage, she published her memoirs in England.

Nancy Hart:
She gathered information on federal movements and led rebels to their positions. Captured, she tricked a man into showing her his gun -- then killed him with it to escape.

Laura Ratcliffe:
She helped Colonel Mosby, of Mosby's Rangers elude capture, and passed information and funds by hiding them under a rock near her home.

Colonel Charles Dahnmon Whitt

Loreta Janeta Velazquez:
Her highly dramatic autobiography has come into question, but her story is that she disguised herself as a man and fought for the Confederacy, sometimes "disguising" herself as a woman to spy.

Sharon Gail, who would suspect a woman to be a spy?

Confederate American

Confederate spy in the American Civil War Maria Isabella Boyd. Isabelle Boyd May 9, 1844 to June 11, 1900

Living in Martinsburg, Virginia, Belle Boyd passed information on Union army activities in the Shenandoah area to General T. J. Jackson (Stonewall Jackson). Belle Boyd was captured and imprisoned and released. Belle Boyd then went to England, followed by a Union officer, Capt. Samuel Hardinge, who had guarded her after an earlier capture. She married him and then in 1866 when he died, leaving her with a small daughter to support, she became an actress.

Belle Boyd later married John Swainston Hammond and moved to California, where she gave birth to a son. Fighting mental illness, she moved with Hammond to the Baltimore area, had three more sons. The family moved to Dallas, Texas, and she divorced Hammond and married a young actor, Nathaniel Rue High. In 1886 they moved to Ohio and Belle Boyd began to appear on stage in a Confederate uniform to talk about her time as a spy.

Belle Boyd died in Wisconsin, where she is buried.

Her book, *Belle Boyd in Camp and Prison,* is an embellished version of her exploits as a spy in the American Civil War.

Colonel Charles Dahnmon Whitt

Antonia Ford 1838 to 1871 was a Confederate Spy.

She lived at the home owned by her father, Edward R. Ford, located across the road from the Fairfax Courthouse. General J.E.B. Stuart was an occasional visitor at the home, as was his scout, John Singleton Mosby.

Federal troops occupied Fairfax in 1861 and Antonia Ford passed along to Stuart information on troop activity. Gen. Stuart gave her a written honorary commission as an aide decamps for her help. On the basis of this paper, she was arrested as a Confederate spy. She was imprisoned in Old Capital Prison in Washington, D.C.

Major Joseph C. Willard, a co-owner of the Willard Hotel in Washington, D.C., who had been a provost marshal at the Fairfax Courthouse, negotiated for Ford's release from prison. He then married her.

She was credited with helping plan the Confederate raid on the Fairfax County Courthouse, although Mosby and Stuart denied her help. She has also been credited with driving her carriage 20 miles past federal troops and through rain to report to General Stuart, just before the Second Battle of Manassas/Bull Run (1862) a Union plan to deceive Confederate troops.

Their son, Joseph E. Willard, served as lieutenant governor of Virginia and U.S. minister to Spain. A daughter of Joseph Willard married Kermit Roosevelt.

Confederate American

Rose O'Neal Greenhow 1814 to 1864

Maryland-born Rose O'Neal married the wealthy Virginian Dr. Robert Greenhow and, living in Washington, DC, became a well-known hostess in that city as she raised their four daughters. In 1850, the Greenhows moved to Mexico, then to San Francisco where Dr. Greenhow died of an injury, leaving Rose widowed.

The widowed Rose O'Neal Greenhow moved back to Washington, DC, and resumed her role as a popular social hostess with many political and military contacts. At the start of the Civil War, she began supplying her Confederate friends with information gleaned from her pro-Union contacts.

One important piece of information that Greenhow passed along was the timetable for the Union Army's movements towards Manassas in 1861, which allowed General Beauregard to gather enough forces before the forces joined battle in the First Battle of Bull Run / Manassas, July 1861.

Allan Pinkerton, head of the detective agency and of the federal government's new secret service, became suspicious of Greenhow, and had her arrested and her home searched in August. Maps and documents were found and she was placed under house arrest. When it was discovered that she was still managing to pass information to the Confederate espionage network, she was taken to the Old Capital Prison in Washington, DC,

Colonel Charles Dahnmon Whitt

and imprisoned with her youngest daughter, Rose. Here, again, she was able to continue to gather and pass along information.

Finally, in May, 1862, Greenhow was sent to Richmond, where she was greeted as a heroine. She was appointed to a diplomatic mission in England and France that summer, and she published her memoirs, *My Imprisonment and the First Year of Abolition Rule at Washington*, as part of the propaganda effort to bring England into the war on the side of the Confederacy.

Returning to America in 1864, Greenhow was on the blockade runner Condor when it was chased by a Union ship and ran aground on a sandbar at the mouth of the Cape Fear River in a storm. She asked to be put into a lifeboat, along with $2,000 in gold sovereigns that she was carrying, to avoid capture; instead, the stormy sea and the heavy load swamped the boat and she was drowned. She was given a full military funeral and buried in Wilmington, North Carolina.

Nancy Hart also known as: Nancy Douglas was born about 1841

Living in Nicholas County, then in Virginia and now part of West Virginia, Nancy Hart joined the Moccasin Rangers and served as a spy, reporting on federal troop activity in her home's vicinity and leading rebel raiders to their position. She was said to have led a raid on Summersville in July 1861, at age 18. Captured by a band of Union soldiers, she tricked one of her captors and used his own gun to kill him, then escaped. After the war she married Joshua Douglas.

Confederate American

Laura Ratcliffe was born about 1836 and served as a Spy for the South

Her home was in the Frying Pan area, Fairfax County, Virginia, was sometimes used as a headquarters by CSA Col. John Singleton Mosby of Mosby's Rangers during the American Civil War.

Early in the war, Laura Ratcliffe discovered a Union plan to capture Mosby and notified him of it so that he could elude capture. When Mosby captured a large cache of federal dollars, he had her hold the money for him. She used a rock near her home to conceal messages and money for Mosby.

Laura Ratcliffe was also associated with Major General J.E.B. Stuart.

Although it was obvious that her home was the center of Confederate activity, she was never arrested or formally charged for her activities.

She married Milton Hanna.

Colonel Charles Dahnmon Whitt

Loreta Velazquez was a Confederate Spy, born about 1842

According to *"The Woman in Battle,"* a book published by Loreta Velazquez in 1876 and the main source for her story. Her father was the owner of plantations in Mexico and Cuba and a Spanish government official, and her mother's parents were a French naval officer and the daughter of a wealthy American family.
Loreta Velazquez claimed four marriages (though never took any of her husbands' names). Her second husband enlisted in the Confederate army at her urging and when he left for duty, she raised a regiment for him to command. He died in an accident, and the widow then enlisted -- in disguise -- and served at Manassas/Bull Run, Ball's Bluff, Fort Donelson and Shiloh under the name Lieutenant Harry T. Buford.
Source: Joan Johnson Lewis

How else could women be used as weapons?
(Only a few women would fit in this category, most southern women were Christian upright ladies.)
"General Hooker's men frequented the Harlots so much; they gave them the name of "Hookers!"

Since the time of Adam and Eve, man has become the weaker sex when the woman is *"Enticing."* What then is a better way to weaken the Northern Soldiers? Some folks think that the infected Harlots of Tennessee were sent upon the Yankee army.

It is hardly a startling notion that during war the incidence of sexual prostitution rises in the proximity of armies.

Confederate American

What is unusual and completely unique, however, was the reaction to the problem in the Volunteer State during the Civil War.

America's first legal systems of prostitution were established in Nashville and Memphis by the US Army Medical Corps in an effort to reduce the high numbers of cases of venereal diseases among soldiers. <u>Such diseases were a threat to the fighting ability of the army and had to be controlled.</u> But the system was established neither overnight nor without trial and error. After all nothing of the sort had ever been attempted in the country and certainly not by the U.S. Army. The management of organized prostitution through legalization is infrequently acknowledged as having much place in Civil War history, but forms one of the more fascinating stories of the conflict in Tennessee.

Since Confederate forces left no record of the presence of prostitution it might appear Southern soldiers adhered to a higher moral standard than lustful Yankees. The moral judgment is probably not the least bit true, but that the Confederate record does not seem to point to problems of prostitution is most likely a function of the fact that Tennessee's cities were occupied by the Union Army long before the problem of venereal disease manifested itself. But there is some, albeit admittedly inadequate, information regarding prostitution within rebel lines. For example, on May 12, 1864, Captain Russ B. Davis, 10th Tennessee (US) reported on the results of a scout through Hickman and Maury Counties. Davis had captured two guerrillas after which his lieutenant had learned of two more guerrillas. He picked up their trail and pursued them o'er hill and dale until finally he was upon

Colonel Charles Dahnmon Whitt

them, they being concealed in a house of ill repute situated in a most secluded spot on the top of a large bluff. The lieutenant, fearing escape on their part, dashed upon them alone and shot them both before any of his party were on the spot.

Nashville's red-light district had been around from at least the 1840s, and there had been unsuccessful efforts made to eliminate it. In 1854, for example, the city government passed an ordinance which had the effect of removing prostitutes from *"the lower part of the city,"* but only after two-weeks notice was given. The law, however, did nothing to eliminate prostitution and by the eve of the Civil War the city's red-light district was thriving near the river in a two by four block wide quarter. The district no doubt was the scene of many a ribald celebration during the heady days of secession and continued to prosper under Confederate rule. The occupation of the state capitol by the Union army in February, 1862, only increased the size of the district's population and did nothing to eliminate it. By the spring of 1863 the district, now given the name *"Smoky Row,"* had become a problem to Union commanders. General R.S. Granger, commanding Federal forces in the city, was by that time *"daily and almost hourly beset"* by regimental commanders and surgeons to take action *"to save the army from a fate worse than to perish on the battlefield."* It was both a health and a moral problem because a sick army could not fight and prostitution was *"annoying and destructive to the morals of the army."* <u>Prostitution was as much a threat to the Union Army as was the Confederate army. Whether on purpose or not, the southern harlots were aiding the Confederacy.</u>
On July 6, 1863, therefore, the round-up of all prostitutes began by order of U.S. Army Provost Marshall Lieutenant Colonel George Spalding. The "Cyprians," (Harlots) as the

Confederate American

prostitutes were called, were to be sent on a forced exile. Their removal was a military necessity and the military response was quick.

According to one newspaper account: *"Squads of soldiers were engaged in heaping furniture out of the various dens, and then tumbling their discontented owners after."* Some 300 were arrested and held for exile. They were sent north to Cincinnati on board the steamship, Idaho, a newly built passenger steamer commandeered for the task. In their absence, partly as a result of the influx of contraband into the city and the lack of competition, black prostitutes soon took the place of their exiled white sisters. One newspaper editor hoped *"that, while in the humor of ridding our town of the libidinous white women, General Granger will dispose of the hundreds of black ones who are making our fair city a Gomorrah."*

Apparently, the Black Harlots were not similarly rounded up. To the contrary, the streets of Nashville were *"Then thare was an old saying that no man could be a soldier unless he had gone through Smoky Row....I went with them and of all the sights you could see. I dare not tell you but I believe the street was about three fourths of a mile long and Every house or Shanty on Boath Sides was a house of Ill-repute. Women had no thought as to Dress or Decency. They Said Smokey Row killed more Yankee Soldiers than the war."*

The white and colored southern harlots were glad to lay with the Union Troops for the money and to give them the weakening diseases of vice! Source: James B. Jones Jr.

Colonel Charles Dahnmon Whitt

Chapter 18

Economy of the Confederate States of America

Source: Wikipedia, the free encyclopedia

The Confederate States of America had an agriculture based economy that relied heavily on slave-worked plantations for the production of cotton for export to Europe and the northern US States. If ranked as an independent nation, it would have been the fourth richest country of the world in 1860. When the Union blockaded its ports in the summer 1861, exports of cotton fell 95 percent and the South had to restructure itself to emphasize food production and munitions production. After losing control of its main rivers and ports, it had to depend on a rickety railroad system that, with few repairs, no new equipment and federal raids, crumbled away. The financial infrastructure collapsed during the war as inflation destroyed banks and forced a move toward a barter economy for civilians. The government seized needed supplies and livestock. By 1865 the economy was in ruins.

Agriculture;

The main agricultural products of the Confederate States were cotton, tobacco, and sugar cane, with some cattle and much grain. In 1862, there was a severe drought that, despite efforts to switch from cotton planting to grain farming, caused food shortages and even bread riots in the winter of 1862 and spring of 1863. The harvests in the

Confederate American

Confederate States were fairly plentiful after 1862, but often went to waste as they could not be harvested or moved to markets. Corn was raised in large quantities and in general, the raising of food products instead of tobacco and cotton was encouraged by legislation and otherwise.

The scarcity of food in the armies and cities was due mostly to the shortage of male labor caused by conscription (The Draft), the disruption of transportation and finance, and the fact that important regions farmland were turned into battlefields, where armies from both sides quickly took all available food and animals. Compounding the problem was the ever increasing number of refugees flooding into cities. Food distribution became increasingly harder and at times, impossible.

(Refer back to Chapter 6 for more on Railroads.) The progressive destruction of the southern railroad network, along with rapid inflation, hit women in the cities especially hard as they found food prices to be too high to afford. This could be seen in the infamous Richmond bread riots of April, 1863, when a large mob of starving women in the city looted stores for food, ignoring the pleas of President Jefferson Davis who stood upon a cart to address the mob, and only dispersed when he threatened for a company of militia to open fire. This and other stories of hardship on the home front greatly demoralized Confederate soldiers when they received letters from their wives, and hence *"thousands of husbands discharged themselves"* to save their families over the course of the war.

Colonel Charles Dahnmon Whitt

Despite the Confederacy's strength in cotton production, it produced very little wool for winter clothing, and by the end of the first year, its most productive regions were in the hands of the Union. Instead it was mostly reliant upon foreign sources. The planting of opium, required for morphine and other medicines was encouraged but did not yield significant quantities.

Manufacturing;

The Confederacy's industrial workforce, like its agricultural workforce, was characterized by its wide and extensive use of slaves. In the 1850s, anywhere from 150,000 - 200,000 slaves were used in industrial work. Most, almost 4/5, were owned directly by industrial owners, the other being bonded out by plantation owners. Often, manual labor performed by slaves would be combined with skilled white workers in order to better compete with northern and foreign industry.

Despite the profitability of slave workers, Southern industry had been under capitalized for years by the time of the outbreak of the war. Besides a social preference for ownership of real property. Agriculture in staple goods was considered the easiest route to making profit. Thus agriculture always outbid industry when it came to capital allocation. As early as 1830, Southern industry was a generation behind, and by the Civil War, was vastly inferior to northern and foreign manufacturing.

Shipbuilding;

At the outset of hostilities, only two government owned naval yards were located in the south. Of private shipyards, anywhere from 36-145 existed, of varying tonnage and skill. While sawmills were readily available to

Confederate American

supply the construction of wooden boats, iron processing in the south was limited.

Textiles;

In the initial volleys of the war, the Confederate government sought the use of handmade and homebased industry to fulfill manufacture of finished textile goods, such as shirts and shoes. Finding this method of production inadequate, the government moved to consolidate finished-goods production into military run textile shops concentrated in larger cities. These textile shops, with the exception of those captured or destroyed, continued to run until the end of the war. Private mills generally supplied raw textiles to these shops for refinement.

Protected from northern and European imports by the blockade, however, privately owned textile mills found themselves in a very lucrative market. Ever rising prices due to scarcity and high levels of demand made sales to the public far more profitable than fixed price contract sales to the military. So much so, that in the first year private mills often refused or cut back on fulfillments ordered by Confederate quartermasters. The advent of conscription,(The Draft) giving the government complete control over the labor force, as well as control over railroads and other forms of transport, precluded such avoidance.

Government Control;

The only manufactures over which the confederate government sought control were those which directly

Colonel Charles Dahnmon Whitt

supplied the needs of the army. These were two classes: (1)arms and munitions, which were under the charge of the ordinace bureau; and (2) a more diverse group which included clothing, blankets, tents, shoes, wagons, saddles, and harness, which for the most part were provided by the quartermaster's bureau.

Source: Charles W. Ramsdell

While the general political sentiment in the Confederacy was reluctance towards government involvement in private business, the extreme needs of the war forced the Confederate government to exert a strong control over industry related to war aims. The bureau of conscription, empowered by the conscription act of 1862 and 1863, dispensed exemptions to those in industry, if necessary, provided a powerful incentive to private industry to fulfill government contracts. If an owner refused, they would find themselves quickly without their labor force, <u>free or slaves.</u>

Navigation;

Before the war the South had a good system of transportation by riverboats on a huge network of navigable rivers, plus a dozen ocean ports. In May 1861 the Union naval blockade shut down almost all port activity except for blockade runners. International and coastal traffic fell 90 percent or more. In peacetime, the vast system of navigable rivers allowed for cheap and easy transportation of farm products. The vast geography made for difficult Union control and Union Soldiers were used to guard captured areas and protect rail lines. The Union Navy seized most of the navigable rivers by 1862, making its own movements easy and Confederate

Confederate American

movements difficult. After the fall of Vicksburg in July 1863, it became impossible for units to cross the Mississippi since Union gunboats constantly patrolled it. The eastern and western portions of the Confederacy were never reconnected. The Union blockade squeezed the life out of the Confederate States of America.

Railroads;

Confederate railroads in the American Civil War (More information in Chapter 6.) The outbreak of war had a depressing effect on the economic fortunes of the Confederate railroad industry. With the cotton crop being hoarded in an attempt to entice European intervention, railroads were without their main source of income. Many were forced to lay off employees and in particular, let go skilled technicians and engineers. For the early years of the war, the Confederate government had a hands off approach to the railroads. It wasn't until middle of 1863 that the Confederate government initiated an overall policy and it was confined solely to aiding the war effort. With the legislation of takeover the same year, rail roads and their rolling stock, came under the control of the military.

In the last year before the end of the war, the Confederate railroad system was always on the verge of collapse. The control policy of Quartermaster's ran the rails ragged. Feeder lines would be scrapped in order to lay down replacement steel for trunk lines, and the continual use of rolling stock wore them down faster than they could be replaced.

Colonel Charles Dahnmon Whitt

Export;

The states that entered the Confederate States accounted for 70 percent of total US exports, and the Confederate leaders believed that this would give the new nation a firm financial basis. Cotton was the primary potential export, accounting for 75 percent of Southern goods either shipped to northern US states or exported in 1860. The Confederate States entered the war with the hope that its near monopoly of the world cotton trade would force the European importing countries, especially Great Britain and France, to intervene in the war on her behalf. In 1861, Southerners at the local level imposed an embargo on cotton shipments; it was not the government's policy. Millions of bales of cotton went unshipped, and by summer 1861 the blockade closed down all normal trade.

A small fraction of the cotton was exported through blockade runners. In the total course of the war, 446,000 bales of cotton were exported to England and Europe. Ironically, the largest amount of cotton exports went to the United States. Most cotton however, would never be traded during the Confederacy's existence, either being destroyed during the war or hoarded till the end. They should have sold when they could.

Disputes over the proper tariff rate had been a sectional political issue between northern and southern states at one point almost leading to a prior dissolution of the Union. Southerners mostly opposed protectionist tariffs for finished goods, fearing they would lessen the value of their raw material exports, as foreign manufactures would be blocked from sales back to the United States. Southern political pressure kept the tariffs at low levels from 1847 through 1860. The founders of the Confederate States did away with this opposition in the Confederate States

Confederate American

Constitution with a prohibition of protectionist tariffs. One of the first acts of the Confederate Congress was the lowering of import tariffs from the then current US average rate of 20 percent to 10 percent. (Another reason to leave the Union.)

However the Confederacy proposed to impose its tariffs on all imports from the USA, which would have been a vast increase in taxes for the Southerners. Almost no tariffs were collected; the total customs revenue collected was about $3.3 million (Confederate dollars), from 1861 through 1864.

Import;

The seceded South, even before the outbreak of hostilities, was faced with the necessity of securing the basic materials of war. They lacked guns, cannon, and munitions of every sort; it lacked most of the raw materials from which they could be manufactured. The South needed clothing, medicine, tools, and, later on, food. It lacked the factories to manufacture the provisions of war and the machinery and skilled labor with which to establish and run factories. As a result the Confederacy, at the very start, turned it eyes towards Europe."

Source: William Diamond

Just as the blockade had made export of Confederate goods prohibitive, so did it frustrate the imports of vital goods to the Confederate war effort. Importers often had to use transshipment points, (such as ports in the Caribbean,) transferring and splitting cargo onto smaller ships for the final leg. Thus shipments became sporadic

Colonel Charles Dahnmon Whitt

and delayed. In the immediate aftermath of Fort Sumter, agents headed by Major Caleb Huse, were sent abroad to Europe to procure weapons and other necessary supplies. Despite these efforts, the first shipment did not leave England until August, and didn't arrive in the South till November, a full 8 months after the outbreak of hostilities. The slow rate of importation continued from September 1861 to February 1862, with a grand total of 15,000 small arms procured for the Confederate Army. After February the Confederacy's fortunes in weapons procurement changed dramatically. From April 1862 till August of that year the Confederacy was able to procure some 48,150 arms, over three times the amount gained in the same period the year before. By February 1863, the total number of guns purchased had raised to a total of 174,129. While some of these weapons were caught by the Union Navy in the blockade, a slight majority made it through, with 40.9 percent of all privateers being caught in 1862.

Raw minerals that the South was in need of were acquired through trade with Mexico, mostly sulphur, copper, powder, and niter. Union officials recognized the extent of trade with Mexico and aggressively tried to interrupt it. Despite their efforts and the fall of the Mississippi River into Union hands the flow of goods from Mexico to the Confederacy was unabated until the end of the war. While attempts were made to engage shipbuilders on the Pacific coast, in an attempt to access ports in South America, none of the plans came to pass. Only the Confederate Steamer, the Alabama, after finding the Atlantic too hostile, set sail for Pacific waters in an attempt to wreck America's Far-East trade. Though it succeeded in its mission to harass American trade interests, it did not manage to open new ports or engage

Confederate American

in trade for the Confederacy, and it was sunk before it could return home with its captured goods.

Blockade runners who sold to the public dealt almost exclusively in luxury and other high profit items, despite the ever present need for staple goods. The practice became so outlandish that the Confederate congress came to ban the import of luxury items, though the law was not effectively enforced. Smuggling over land, from either Mexico or Union territory, also provided a profitable trade in luxury items, though it also become a useful means of acquiring much needed medicine.

Currency;

The holdings of the banks largely found their way into the Confederate treasury in payment for a $15,000,000 loan effected early in 1861. These sums were soon sent to Europe in payment of foreign war supplies. The gold and silver in general circulation also soon left the Confederate States of America almost entirely, driven out by the rising flood of paper money. Aside from the payment of the above loan, the government never secured any revenue, and was driven headlong into the wholesale issue of paper money. The first notes were issued in March 1861, and bore interest. They were soon followed by others, bearing no interest and payable in two years, others payable six months after peace. New issues were continually provided, so that from an initial $1,000,000 in circulation in July 1861, the amount rose to $30 million before December 1861; to $100 million by March 1862; to $200 million by August 1862; to perhaps $450 million by December 1862; to $700 million by the autumn of 1863; and to a much larger figure before the end of the war.

Colonel Charles Dahnmon Whitt
$15 bond coupon circulated as cash, but depreciated rapidly in value

This policy of issuing irredeemable paper money was

copied by the individual states and other political bodies. Alabama began by issuing $1,000,000 in notes in February 1861, and added to this amount during each subsequent session of the state legislature. The other states followed suit. Cities also sought to replenish their treasuries in the same way. Corporations and other business concerns tried to meet the rising tide of prices with the issue of their individual promissory notes intended to circulate from hand to hand.

As a result of this redundancy of the currency, its value collapsed. Gold was quoted at a premium in Confederate notes in April 1861. By the end of that year, a paper dollar was quoted at 90 cents in gold; during 1862 that figure fell to 40 cents; during 1863, to 6 cents; and still lower during the last two years of the war. The downward course of this figure, with occasional recoveries, reflects the popular estimate of the Confederacy's chance of winning independence. The lack of trade was the downfall.

Confederate American

The oversupply of currency drove the price of commodities to exorbitant heights and disarranged all business. Savings in nominal dollars lost 90 percent or more of their value. It affected different classes of commodities differently. Imports like coffee became very expensive, and substitutes were found. (Massey 1952) Confederate asset price stabilization policies appear to have increased the velocity of circulation and countered productivity that channeled inflationary pressures into other areas of the economy. Three successive monetary reforms encouraged holders of treasury notes to exchange these notes for bonds by imposing deadlines on their convertibility. Confederate legislative efforts aimed at starting the conversion of currency into bonds did temporarily suppress currency depreciation. These acts also triggered rises in commodity prices, however, because note holders rushed to spend the currency before their exchange rights were reduced.

Speculators were continually policed for importing high priced luxuries instead of confining themselves to supplying the government with foreign war supplies. Tobacco and cotton, which found few foreign buyers owing to the blockade, actually fell in value as quoted in gold. The great differences of the price of these two commodities in the CSA and abroad. The New York price of cotton increased more than ten times more then old value during the war. This offered the strongest inducement to evade the blockade and export them. A small amount of cotton reached the world market by way of the Atlantic ports or Mexico, and netted those concerned in the venture handsome profits. By 1862, Federal Treasury agents from Washington were buying cotton, offering very large sums for planters willing to do

Colonel Charles Dahnmon Whitt

business with the enemy. Tobacco and cotton were smuggled through the military lines in exchange for hospital stores, coffee, and similar articles. The military authorities tried to suppress this illicit trade, but at times even they were carried away by the desire to secure the much desired foreign supplies.

The disturbances of prices, their local differences and fluctuations, produced wild speculation in the Confederate States. Normal business was almost impossible and a gambling element was forced into every transaction. Speculation in gold was especially pronounced. Legislation and popular feeling were aimed at it, but without avail. Even the government itself was compelled to speculate in gold. Speculation in food and other articles was equally inevitable. Laws were formed to curb the speculators, but had no effect.

The policy of the Confederate banks during the war encouraged speculation. The New Orleans banks had been well managed and remained solvent until September 1861. The banks of the other states suspended coin payments at the end of 1860 and thereafter enlarged their note issue and their loans, thereby adding to the general redundancy of the currency and stimulating the prevalent speculative craze. They did a large business by speculating in cotton, making advances to the planters on the basis of their crops. The state governments also used their note issues for this purpose. The planters urgently demanding relief as their cotton could not reach a market. The Confederate government also made advances on cotton and secured large quantities by purchase, to serve as the basis of cotton bonds. The rise in prices which reflected the redundancy of the currency was no advantage to the producer. Frequent efforts were made by legislation and otherwise to reduce the prices

Confederate American

demanded, especially by the planters. As a result the production of food products fell off, or at least the farmers did not bring their products to market for fear of being forced to sell them at a loss. Supplies for the army were obtained by pressure; the price to be paid for them being fixed at a low figure. As a result, the army administration found it almost impossible to induce producers of food willingly to turn over their products, and the army suffered from want. (Who's side were these planters on?) Under these confused industrial circumstances, the sufferings of the debtor class were loudly asserted, and laws were passed to relieve them of their burdens, making the collection of debts difficult or impossible. The debts of Southerners to Northerners contracted before the war were confiscated by the Confederate Government, but did not amount to a large figure.

Confederate war finance;

The effectiveness of the Union blockade and the peculiar industrial development of the Confederate States removed the possibility of an ample government revenue. Though import duties were levied the proceeds amounted to almost nothing. A small export duty on cotton was expected to produce a large revenue sufficient to base a loan upon, but the small amount of cotton exports reduced this source of revenue to an insignificant figure. With no manufactures to tax under an internal revenue system such as the US Government adopted, the Confederacy was cut off from geting any considerable revenue from indirect taxation. The first Confederate tax law levied a direct tax of twenty million dollars, which was apportioned among the states. These, with the exception of Texas, contributed their apportioned share to the central

Colonel Charles Dahnmon Whitt

government by issuing bonds or notes, so that the tax was in reality but a disguised form of loan. Real taxation was postponed until the spring of 1863, when a stringent measure was adopted taxing property and earnings. It was slowly and with difficulty put into effect, and was reenacted in February 1864. In the states and cities there was a strong tendency to relax or postpone taxation in view of the other demands upon the people.

With no revenue from taxation and with the disastrous effects of the wholesale issue of paper money before it, the Confederate government made every effort to borrow money by issuing bonds. The initial $15 million loan was soon followed by an issue of one hundred million in bonds, which it was difficult to place. This was followed by even larger loans. The bonds rapidly fell in value and were quoted during the war at approximately the value of the paper money, in which medium they were paid for by subscribers. To avoid this circumstance a system of produce loans was devised by which the bonds were subscribed for in cotton, tobacco, and food products. This policy was subsequently enlarged and enabled the government to secure at least a part of the armies' food supplies. But the bulk of the subscriptions for these bonds was made in cotton, for which the planters were then enabled to find a market.

Why did the Confederate government not undertake more external loans? The other, more subtle, potential explanation for a small amount of external borrowing is the issuing of war debt. This presents a moral hazard which rises sharply in the case of the American Confederacy.

Lenders could expect that defeat would result in a huge debt. It was hoped to keep the currency within bounds by

Confederate American

holders of paper money exchanging it for bonds, which the law allowed and encouraged. As notes and bonds fell in value all at once there was no inducement for holders to make that exchange. On the contrary, a note holder had an advantage over a bond holder, in that he could use his currency for speculation or for purchases in general.

In the autumn of 1862, the Confederate law attempted to compel note holders to fund their notes in bonds, in order to reduce the redundancy of the currency and lower prices. Disappointed in the result of this legislation, the Congress, in February 1864, went much farther in the same direction by passing a law requiring note holders to fund their notes before a certain date, after which notes would be taxed a third or more of their face value. This drastic measure was accepted as meaning a partial refusal of the Confederate debt and though it for a time reduced the currency outstanding and lowered prices, it wrecked the government's credit and made it impossible for the Confederate Treasury to float any more loans. During the last months of the war, the ConfederateTreasury led a most odd existence and its actual operations can only be surmised.

During the entire war the notion that the CSA possessed a most efficient engine of war in its monopoly of cotton *(the "King Cotton" idea)* buoyed up the hopes of the Confederates. The government strained every effort to secure recognition of the Confederacy as a nation by the great powers of Europe. It also was successfully in securing individual foreigners' financial recognition of the Confederate States by effecting a foreign loan based on cotton. This favorite notion was put into practice in the

Colonel Charles Dahnmon Whitt

spring of 1863. The French banking house of Erlanger & Company undertook to float a loan of $3,000,000, redeemable after the war in cotton at the rate of sixpence a pound. As cotton at the time was selling at nearly four times that figure, and would presumably be quoted far above sixpence long after the establishment of peace. The bonds offered strong attractions to those speculatively inclined and in sympathy with the Confederate cause. The placing of the bonds in Europe was mismanaged by the Confederate agents, but notwithstanding, a considerable sum was secured from the public and used for the purchase of naval and military stores. At the close of the war these foreign bonds were ignored by the re-established Federal authorities like all the other bonds of the Confederate Government or of state governments under the Confederacy.

So as you can see, the Union Blockade caused scarcity and inflation. This once rich land was sant into poverty. Only stuborn loyalty of the half starved soldiers and the great leadership of Robert E. Lee was the Confederacy able to last for four long years.

Confederate American
Chapter 19
Confederates and God

Source: Gordon Leidner of Great American History

During the American Civil War, several significant spiritual revivals took place in both the northern and southern armies. (Both Armies thought that God was with them.)

Before the Revivals

The early months of the American Civil War saw the assembly of armies that consisted of thousands of young men that had never before been away from home. Army chaplains complained that *"seductive influences of sin"* and *"legions of devils"* infested the camps. Among the sins were *"spirituous liquors," card playing, gambling, and profanity.* Early in the war, one Confederate soldier said that *"if the South is overthrown, the epitaph should be "died of whiskey."*

Abraham Lincoln recognized the value of religion as a stabilizing force in the Union army, and did all within his power to provide for organized spiritual guidance to soldiers. On May 4, 1861, he ordered all regimental commanders to appoint chaplains for their units. The Chaplain was expected to be an ordained minister of a

Colonel Charles Dahnmon Whitt

Christian denomination, and was to receive an officer's salary (initially $1,700 per year, later cut to $1,200). Lincoln also provided as much support as he could to the United States Christian Commission, an inter-denominational organization that was dedicated primarily to the spreading of the Gospel in the Union armies.

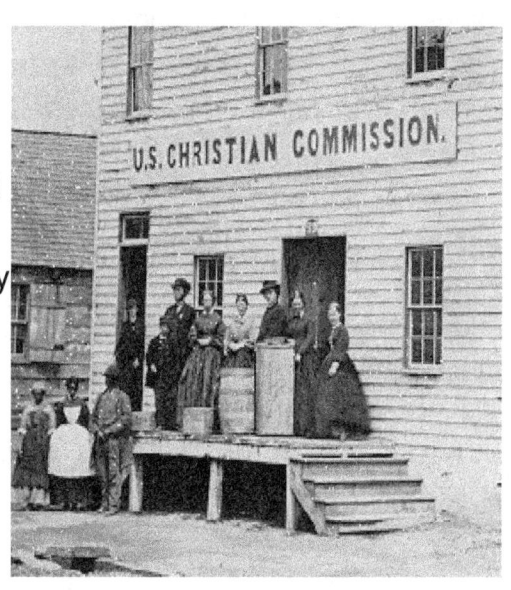

Unfortunately for the southern soldiers, Jefferson Davis and his administration put less value on the establishment of army chaplains and evangelistic activities within the army. There was no corresponding effort to assure that every regiment had a chaplain and those that were appointed received a salary initially of $1,020 per year, which was soon reduced to $600. Although the salary was later increased to $960, few Confederate army chaplains were ever fully supported by the Confederate authorities. The Confederate government was more anxious to have *"fighting men"* than *"preaching men."*

Southern Christian leaders, usually via their respective denominational organizations, made earnest efforts to

Confederate American

provide the soldiers with Bibles, New Testaments, and religious tracts. Those chaplains and religious leaders that lived with the soldiers sent out a constant stream of letters to their home churches and church leadership, begging them to send "our best men--holy men" to assist in evangelizing and ministering to the troops. Although the South had few facilities for printing its own Bibles, southern Christian leaders put forward supreme efforts to acquire Bibles and tracts for their soldiers. British and even some northern Bible societies responded generously.

Northern soldiers were fortunate in that northern Christian leaders were better organized and more willing to ignore their denominational differences from the very start. With the support of both the Lincoln administration and the War Department, they organized the U.S. Christian Commission--a civilian "army" of men and women that lived in or near the army camps, passing out religious tracts and Testaments, organizing worship services, acting as nurses in the hospitals, and doing their best to spread the Gospel.

A Great Movement of the Holy Spirit

Although the Davis administration was not as supportive of organized religion as it could have been, many of the Confederate military leaders were superb. Of particular note are Generals Robert E. Lee, T. J. "Stonewall"

Colonel Charles Dahnmon Whitt

Jackson, and Leonidas Polk. Lee and Jackson did all within their power to encourage the spreading of the Gospel in the Army of Northern Virginia. Jackson himself encouraged the troops to keep the Sabbath holy and attend worship services. He would usually try to avoid battle on the Sabbath, or, if not possible to do so, would try to set aside a subsequent day of rest. Jackson was frequently seen in prayer--both before and during battle. He always acknowledged God as the author of his military victories

Similarly, Union General George B. McClellan decreed that the North's "holy cause" justified divine services every Sunday morning that military necessity would allow. Union  General Oliver O. Howard, commonly referred to as "the Christian General," would himself preach to the troops when a regular chaplain or minister was not available. In the West, Union General William Rosecrans, a devout Catholic, made it a policy to never fight on Sundays. Even during the battle of Stone's River, after fighting a desperate battle all day on Saturday, he rested his army on Sunday before re-engaging the enemy on Monday.

Confederate American

God evidently honored Rosecran's faithfulness, as the Confederate army retreated.

Although revivals took place throughout the war, it was during the late fall of 1863 through the spring and summer of 1864 that what was subsequently called the "Great Revival" occurred. Although this event is best documented for Lee's Army of Northern Virginia, it actually took place in both northern and southern armies in both the Virginia and the Tennessee theatres of the war.

According to J. William Jones, Confederate Chaplain and author of one of the best documentaries of the Great Revival, virtually every Confederate brigade was affected--and approximately ten percent of the soldiers in the Army of Northern Virginia accepted Christ. Night after night troops participated in prayer meetings, worshipped, and listened to ministers proclaim the good news. Virtually every gathering ended with soldiers coming forward to accept Christ or receive prayer. When a pond or river was nearby, the soldiers would frequently step forward for baptisms, regardless of how cold the weather was.

During the revival, Jones told of how Confederate soldiers would form *"reading clubs,"* in which soldiers would pass around a well-worn Bible, sharing the Gospel. Always hungry for scarce Testaments and religious tracts, the soldiers would see Jones approaching camp and cry out *"Yonder comes the Bible and Tract man!"* and run up to

Colonel Charles Dahnmon Whitt

him and beg for Bibles and Testaments *"as if they were gold guineas for free distribution."* Jones would quickly exhaust his supply of reading material, and sadly have to turn away most of the men. "I have never seen more diligent Bible-readers than we had in the Army of Northern Virginia."

U. S. Christian Commission records show that similar events were happening in the North's principle eastern army, the Army of the Potomac, at the same time. Brigade chapels were so full that many men were frequently turned away. One Union general wrote that he had never seen *"a better state of feeling in religious matters"* in the Army of Potomac.

In the fall and winter of 1863, the Union army in Chattanooga, Tennessee had been besieged by a strong Confederate force, strongly entrenched in the mountains around the city. The Union soldiers were deeply affected by the revival, and many attributed their surprising victory over the Confederates as "a visible interposition of God." Soon after their victory at Chattanooga, the Union troops were pursuing their enemy as they retreated towards Atlanta. The fires of revival continued for the Union troops in Ringgold, Georgia, where hundreds of men were baptized in Chickamauga Creek.

The Confederate's Army of the Tennessee, retreating towards Atlanta, had also experienced the fires of the Great Revival. During their retreat from Dalton, Georgia,

Confederate American

Rev. C. W. Miller tells of a Confederate brigade called together for worship in a field. They read the Bible aloud, sang a song of praise, and began to pray. While one of the soldiers was praying aloud, and his comrades were kneeling in silence, they all heard the distant report of artillery and were soon greeted with the burst of a 32-pound cannon shell overhead. More shells shrieked towards them, and shrapnel fell nearby, but the men continued their prayers as if there was no danger. Finally the chaplain pronounced the benediction and everyone calmly sought cover.

Surprisingly, the revivals continued with Sherman's troops as they marched across Georgia and through the Carolinas. When the soldiers stopped for the night, they frequently assembled in local churches and worshipped.

The Fruit of the Spirit

It is estimated that over 100,000 Confederate and somewhere between 100,000 and 200,000 Union troops accepted Christ during the Civil War, roughly ten percent of the men engaged. There are many accounts of the change that took place in the men, both during the war and afterwards, as a result of the many revivals and movement of the Holy Spirit.

One chaplain recounted the sight of changed hearts at Chinbarazo hospital in Richmond, Virginia: *"No sight could*

Colonel Charles Dahnmon Whitt

be more touching than to stand near the chapel and see the wounded and the pale convalescents hobbling and creeping to the place of worship at the sound of the bell."

A Floridian by the name of Major P. B. Bird, when mortally wounded in the trenches of Richmond near the end of the war, considered his relationship with the Lord and said *"But for leaving my wife and children, I should not feel sad at the prospect of dying. There is no cloud between God and me now."*

Soldiers often talked of their mothers. During one prayer meeting, a young soldier cried aloud *"O that my mother was here!"* When asked why he wanted to see his mother, he replied *"Because she has so long been praying for me, and now I have found the Savior."* Another wounded Christian soldier asked a friend to die."
"Tell my mother that I read my Testament and put all my trust in the Lord....I am not afraid

J. W. Jones, traveling through the South after the war, spied a crippled veteran working in a field, guiding a plow with

"I THANK GOD THAT I HAVE ONE ARM LEFT, AND AN OPPORTUNITY OF USING IT FOR THE SUPPORT OF THOSE I LOVE."

Confederate American

his one good arm. Recognizing him as a man he had known in the war, he stopped to talk to him and provide some encouragement. This particular young man had left college and a promising career when the war broke out, had been wounded in battle, and was baptized by Jones during the war. Jones says *"to see him thus, then, his hopes blighted, his fortune wrecked, and his body maimed for life, deeply touched my heart....I shall never forget how the noble fellow, straightening himself up, replied, with a proud smile: 'Oh, Brother Jones that is all right. I thank God that I have one arm left and an opportunity to use it for the support of those I love.'"*

Such is the story of one changed heart. It is typical of many men that lived through our nation's greatest conflict, and met the Lord Jesus Christ along the way.

"More about Soldier worship,"

Source: Charles A. Jennings

"Revivals are among the charter rights of the Church, a revival means a heartbroken pastor. A revival means a church on its knees confessing its sins - the sins of the individual and of the Church - confessing the sins of the times and of the community."

E.M. Bounds

Colonel Charles Dahnmon Whitt

While pastoring in Brunswick, MO, Rev. Bounds officiated the funeral of a seventeen year old boy who was falsely accused and drowned by Union soldiers in the frozen Grand River. He witnessed the merciless execution of 55 non-combatants by Union troops and preached the funeral of one of the on May 10, 1861 Union troops captured the Missouri Arsenal at St. Louis and made prisoners of the State Guard. That afternoon Union Troops murdered twenty-eight civilians in the *St. Louis Massacre*. Witnessing these brutal atrocities and understanding the unconstitutional position of the Federal government, Rev. Bounds refused to sign the *Oath of Allegiance*. Considered as a spy, he was arrested along with 249 others and was imprisoned in the Jefferson Barracks at St. Louis. After enduring despicable prison conditions for a month and a half, he was ordered to leave the state and not to return. As a prisoner he was taken to Memphis on a Federal boat and then to Washington, AR to a prisoner exchange camp. After his release, he walked over 200 miles to Pine Bluff where be bought a mule and continued traveling east in search of his friend, General Sterling Price. On February 7, 1863 he joined the Confederate Army and was assigned to Company B of the Third Missouri Infantry. Rev. Bounds faithfully served his fellow soldiers as chaplain. He did not hide from danger but remained at the front lines of battle. He witnessed first hand all the horrors, fear, pain, agony and death of war. Between campaigns, Chaplain Bounds would conduct religious services in local churches where many civilians and soldiers accepted the bountiful grace of the Savior and were born into the Kingdom of God.

"Man is looking for better methods. God is looking for better men. Men are God's methods." E. M. Bounds

Confederate American

GENERAL ORDERS—No. 59. HEAD-QUARTERS, ARMY OF NORTHERN VIRGINIA.

May 7, 1863.

"With heart-felt gratification the General Commanding expresses to the army his sense of the heroic conduct displayed by officers and men during the arduous operations in which they have just been engaged. Under trying vicissitudes of heat and storm you attacked the enemy, strongly intrenched in the depths of a tangled wilderness, and again on the hills of Fredericksburg, fifteen miles distant, and, by the valor that has triumphed on so many fields, forced him once more to seek safety beyond the Rappahannock. <u>While this glorious victory entitles you to the praise and gratitude of the nation, we are especially called upon to return our grateful thanks to the only giver of victory for the signal deliverance He has wrought. It is, therefore, earnestly recommended that the troops unite on Sunday next in ascribing to the Lord of Hosts the glory due unto His name.</u> Let us not forget in our rejoicing the brave soldiers who have fallen in defense of their country; and while we mourn their loss let us resolve to emulate their noble example. The army and the country alike lament the absence for a time of one to whose bravery, energy, and skill they are so much indebted for success."

General Robert E. Lee

Colonel Charles Dahnmon Whitt

"Prayer is mightier than Cannon!" Colonel Charles Dahnmon Whitt

Confederate American

Chapter 20

Reconstruction

Source: Wikipedia, the free encyclopedia

In the history of the United States, **Reconstruction Era** has two uses; the first covers the entire nation in the period 1865–1877 following the Civil War; the second one, used in this article, covers the transformation of the Southern United States from 1863 to 1877, with the reconstruction of state and society in the former Confederacy. Three amendments to the Constitution affected the entire nation. In the different states, Reconstruction began and ended at different times; federal Reconstruction policies were finally abandoned with the Compromise of 1877.

Reconstruction policies were debated in the North when the war began and commenced in earnest after the Emancipation Proclamation, issued on January 1, 1863. Reconstruction policies were implemented when a Confederate state came under the control of the Union Army. President Abraham Lincoln set up reconstructed governments in several southern states during the war, including Tennessee, Arkansas and Louisiana, and experimented with giving land to ex-slaves in South Carolina. Following Lincoln's assassination, President Andrew Johnson tried to follow Lincoln's lenient policies and appointed new governors in the summer of 1865. Johnson quickly declared that the war goals of national unity and the ending of slavery had been achieved, so

Colonel Charles Dahnmon Whitt

that reconstruction was completed. Republicans in Congress refused to accept Johnson's lenient terms, rejected the new members of Congress selected by the South, and in 1865-66 broke with the president. A sweeping Republican victory in the 1866 Congressional elections in the North gave the Radical Republicans enough control of Congress that they could overide President Johnson's vetoes and began what is called *"Radical reconstruction"* in 1867.

Congress removed the civilian governments in the South in 1867 and put the former Confederacy under the rule of the U.S. Army. The army then conducted new elections in which the freed slaves could vote while those who held leading positions under the Confederacy were denied the vote and could not run for office.

In ten states, coalitions of freedmen, recent arrivals from the North *(Carpetbaggers),* and white Southerners who supported Reconstruction *(Scalawags)* cooperated to form Republican state governments, which introduced various reconstruction programs, offered massive aid to railroads, built public schools, and raised taxes. Conservative opponents charged that Republican regimes were marred by widespread corruption. Violent opposition towards freedmen and whites who supported Reconstruction emerged in numerous localities under the name of the Ku Klux Klan, which led to federal intervention by President Ulysses S. Grant in 1871 that closed down the Klan. Conservative Democrats calling themselves *"Redeemers"* regained control state by state, sometimes using fraud and violence to control state elections. A deep national economic depression following the Panic of 1873 led to major Democratic gains in the North, the collapse of many railroad schemes in the South, and a growing sense of frustration in the North.

Confederate American

The end of Reconstruction was a staggered process, and the period of Republican control ended at different times in different states. With the Compromise of 1877, Army intervention in the South ceased and Republican control collapsed in the last three state governments in the South. This was followed by a period that white Southerners labeled Redemption, which saw the enactment of Jim Crow Laws and (after 1890) the disenfranchisement of most blacks. The white Southerners' memory of Reconstruction played a major role in reinforcing the system of white supremacy and second class citizenship for blacks, known as the age of Jim Crow. The Democratic Party practically monopolized the *"New South"* into the 1960s, when the civil rights and voting rights of Nergos were restored by Congress.

Reconstruction addressed how the eleven seceding states would regain self-government and be reseated in Congress, the civil status of the former leaders of the Confederacy, and the Constitutional and legal status of freedmen, especially their civil rights and whether they should be given the right to vote. Violent controversy erupted throughout the South over these issues.

The laws and constitutional amendments that laid the foundation for the most radical phase of Reconstruction were adopted from 1866 to 1871. By the 1870s, Reconstruction had officially provided freedmen with equal rights under the law, and they were voting and taking political office. Republican legislatures, coalitions of whites and blacks, established the first public school systems in the South. Beginning in 1874, however, there was a rise in white paramilitary organizations, such as the White League and Red Shirts, whose political aim was to

Colonel Charles Dahnmon Whitt

drive out the Republicans. They also disrupted organizing and terrorized blacks to bar them from the polls. From 1873 to 1877, conservative white Democrats (calling themselves *"Redeemers"*) regained power in the states.

In the 1860s and 1870s the terms *"radical"* and *"conservative"* had distinctive meanings. *"Conservatism"* in this context generally indicates the mindset of the ruling white elite, focused on white supremacy. Many leaders had been Whigs and were committed to modernization. Most of the "radical" Republicans in the North were men who believed in free enterprise and industrialization; most were also modernizers and ex-Whigs. The *"Liberal Republicans"* of 1872 shared the same outlook except they were especially opposed to the corruption they saw around President Grant, and believed that the goals had been achieved so that the federal intervention could now end.

Passage of the 13th, 14th, and 15th Amendments are constitutional legacies of Reconstruction. These Reconstruction Amendments established the rights which, through extensive litigation, led to Supreme Court rulings starting in the early 20th century that struck down discriminatory state laws. A *"Second Reconstruction"*, sparked by the Civil Rights Movement, led to civil rights laws in 1964 and 1965 that ensured full civic rights of African Americans.

Confederate American

Material devastation of the South in 1865

The southern economy had been ruined by the war. Charleston, South Carolina: Broad Street, 1865
Further information: History of the Southern United States

Reconstruction played out against a backdrop of a once prosperous economy in ruins. The Confederacy in 1861 had 297 towns and cities with 835,000 people; of these, 162 with 681,000 people were at one point occupied by Union forces. Eleven were destroyed or severely damaged by war action, including Atlanta, Charleston, Columbia, and Richmond; these eleven contained 115,900 people in the 1860 census, or 14% of the urban South. The number of people who lived in the destroyed towns represented just over 1% of the Confederacy's combined urban and rural populations. In addition, 45 court houses were burned (out of 830), destroying the

Colonel Charles Dahnmon Whitt

documentation for the legal relationships in the affected communities.

Farms were in disrepair and the prewar stock of horses, mules and cattle was much depleted. The South's agriculture was not highly mechanized, but the value of farm implements and machinery in the 1860 Census was $81 million and was reduced by 40% by 1870. The transportation infrastructure lay in ruins, with little railroad or riverboat service available to move crops and animals to market.[12] Railroad mileage was located mostly in rural areas and over two-thirds of the South's rails, bridges, rail yards, repair shops and rolling stock were in areas reached by Union armies, which systematically destroyed what they could. Even in untouched areas, the lack of maintenance and repair, the absence of new equipment, the heavy over-use and the deliberate relocation of equipment by the Confederates from remote areas to the war zone ensured the system would be ruined at war's end. Restoring the infrastructure, especially the railroad system, became a high priority for Reconstruction state governments.

The enormous cost of the Confederate war effort took a high toll on the South's economic infrastructure. The direct costs to the Confederacy in human capital, government expenditures, and physical destruction from the Civil War totaled a staggering 3.3 billion dollars. By 1865, the Confederate dollar was worthless due to massive inflation and people in the South had to resort to bartering for goods or using scarce Union dollars. With the emancipation of the southern slaves the entire economy of the South had to be rebuilt. Having lost their enormous investment in slaves, white planters had minimal capital to pay freedman workers to bring in crops. As a result a system of sharecropping was developed where ex-

Confederate American

slaveholders broke up large plantations and rented small lots to the freedmen and their families. The South transformed from a prosperous landed gentry slave holding society into a tenant farming agriculture system. Per capita income for white southerners declined from $125 in 1857 to a low of $80 in 1879. By the end of the 19th century and well into the 20th century the South was locked into a system of economic poverty. How much of this failure was caused by the war remains the subject of debate among economists and historians.

Restoring the South to the Union

A political cartoon of Andrew Johnson and Abraham Lincoln, 1865, entitled "The Rail Splitter At Work Repairing the Union." The caption reads (Johnson): *Take it quietly Uncle Abe and I will draw it closer than ever.*

Colonel Charles Dahnmon Whitt

(Lincoln): *A few more stitches Andy and the good old Union will be mended.*

During the Civil War, the Radical Republican leaders argued that slavery and the Slave Power had to be permanently destroyed, and that all forms of Confederate nationalism had to be suppressed. Moderates said this could be easily accomplished as soon as Confederate armies surrendered and the Southern states repealed secession and accepted the 13th Amendment, most of which happened by December 1865.

President Lincoln was the leader of the moderate Republicans and wanted to speed up Reconstruction and reunite the nation painlessly and quickly. Lincoln formally began Reconstruction in late 1863 with his ten percent plan, which went into operation in several states but which Radicals opposed. Lincoln vetoed the Radical plan, the Wade–Davis Bill of 1864, which was much more strict than the Ten-Percent Plan.

The opposing faction of Radical Republicans were skeptical of Southern intentions and demanded more stringent federal action. Congressman Thaddeus Stevens and Senator Charles Sumner led the Radical Republicans. Sumner argued that secession had destroyed statehood alone, but the Constitution still extended its authority and its protection over individuals, as in the territories. Thaddeus Stevens and his followers viewed secession as having left the states in a status like new territories. The Republicans sought to prevent Southern politicians from "restoring the historic subordination of Negroes". Since slavery was abolished, the three-fifths compromise no longer applied to counting the population of blacks. After the 1870 census, the South would gain numerous additional representatives in

Confederate American

Congress, based on the population of freedmen. One Illinois Republican expressed a common fear that if the South were allowed to simply restore its previous established powers, that the "reward of treason will be an increased representation".

Upon Lincoln's assassination in April 1865, Andrew Johnson of Tennessee, who had been elected with Lincoln in 1864 on the ticket of the National Union Party as the latter's vice president, became president. Johnson rejected the Radical program of harsh, lengthy Reconstruction and instead appointed his own governors and tried to finish reconstruction by the end of 1865. By early 1866, full-scale political warfare existed between Johnson (now allied with the Democrats) and the Radicals; he vetoed laws and issued orders that contradicted Congressional legislation.

Congress rejected Johnson's argument that he had the war power to decide what to do, since the war was over. Congress decided it had the primary authority to decide how Reconstruction should proceed, because the Constitution stated the United States had to guarantee each state a republican form of government. The Radicals insisted that meant Congress decided how Reconstruction should be achieved. The issues were multiple, who should decide, Congress or the president? How should republicanism operate in the South? What was the status of the Confederate states? What was the citizenship status of men who had supported the Confederacy? What was the citizenship and suffrage status of freedmen?

The election of 1866 decisively changed the balance of power, giving the Republicans two-thirds majorities in both

Colonel Charles Dahnmon Whitt

houses of Congress, and enough votes to overcome Johnson's vetoes. They moved to impeach Johnson because of his constant attempts to thwart radical Reconstruction measures, by using the Tenure of Office Act. Johnson was acquitted by one vote, but he lost the influence to shape Reconstruction policy.

The Republican Congress established military districts in the South and used Army personnel to administer the region until new governments loyal to the Union could be established. While Congress temporarily suspended the ability to vote of approximately 10,000 to 15,000 white men who had been Confederate officials or senior officers, constitutional amendments gave full citizenship and suffrage to former slaves.

With the power to vote, freedmen started participating in politics. While many slaves were illiterate, educated blacks (including escaped slaves) moved down from the North to aid them, and natural leaders also stepped forward. They elected white and black men to represent them in constitutional conventions. A Republican coalition of freedmen, southerners supportive of the Union (derisively called *scalawags* by white Democrats) and northerners who had migrated to the South (mostly called *carpetbaggers*, some of whom were returning natives, but were mostly Union veterans), organized to create constitutional conventions. They created new state constitutions to set new directions for southern states.

Loyalty

The issue of loyalty emerged in the debates over the Wade–Davis Bill of 1864. The bill required voters to take the *"ironclad oath"*, swearing they had never supported the Confederacy or been one of its soldiers. Pursuing a

Confederate American

policy of *"malice toward none"* announced in his second inaugural address, Lincoln asked voters only to support the Union. The Radicals lost support following Lincoln's veto of the Wade–Davis Bill but regained strength after Lincoln's assassination in April 1865.

Monument in honor of the Grand Army of the Republic, organized after the war

Suffrage

Congress had to consider how to restore to full status and representation within the Union those southern states that had declared their independence from the United States and had withdrawn their representation. Suffrage for former Confederates was one of two main concerns. A decision needed to be made whether to allow just some or all former Confederates to vote (and to hold office). The moderates wanted virtually all of them to vote, but the Radicals resisted. They repeatedly tried to impose the

Colonel Charles Dahnmon Whitt

ironclad oath, which would effectively have allowed no former Confederates to vote. Representative Thaddeus Stevens of Pennsylvania proposed, unsuccessfully, that all former Confederates lose the right to vote for five years. The compromise that was reached disenfranchised many former Confederate civil and military leaders. No one knows how many temporarily lost the vote, but one estimate was 10,000 to 15,000.

Second, and closely related, was the issue of whether freedmen should be allowed to vote. The issue was how to receive the four million former slaves as citizens. If they were to be fully counted as citizens, some sort of representation for apportionment of seats in Congress had to be determined. Before the war, the population of slaves had been counted as three-fifths of a comparable number of free whites. By now having the benefit of four million freedmen counted as full citizens, the South would gain additional seats in Congress. If blacks were denied the vote and the right to hold office, then only whites would represent them. Many conservatives, including most white southerners, northern Democrats, and some northern Republicans, opposed black voting. Some northern states that had referendums on the subject limited the ability of their own small populations of blacks to vote.

Lincoln had supported a middle position to allow some black men to vote, especially army veterans. Johnson also believed that such service should be rewarded with citizenship. Lincoln proposed giving the vote to *"the very intelligent, and especially those who have fought gallantly in our ranks."* In 1864, Governor Johnson said, *"The better class of them will go to work and sustain themselves, and that class ought to be allowed to vote, on the ground that a loyal negro is more worthy than a*

Confederate American

disloyal white man." As President in 1865, Johnson wrote to the man he appointed as governor of Mississippi, recommending, *"If you could extend the elective franchise to all persons of color who can read the Constitution in English and write their names, and to all persons of color who own real estate valued at at least two hundred and fifty dollars, and pay taxes thereon, you would completely disarm the adversary [Radicals in Congress], and set an example the other states will follow."*

Senators Charles Sumner of Massachusetts and Thaddeus Stevens, leaders of the Radical Republicans, were initially hesitant to enfranchise the largely illiterate former slave population. Sumner preferred at first impartial requirements that would have imposed literacy restrictions on blacks and whites. He believed, however, that he would not succeed in passing legislation to disfranchise illiterate whites who already had the vote.

In the South, many poor whites were illiterate. In 1880, for example, the white illiteracy rate was about 25% in Tennessee, Kentucky, Alabama, South Carolina, and Georgia; and as high as 33% in North Carolina. This compares with the 9% national rate and a black rate of illiteracy that was over 70% in the South. By 1900, with emphasis within the black community on education, however, the majority of blacks had achieved literacy.

Sumner soon concluded that *"there was no substantial protection for the freedman except in the franchise."* This was necessary, he stated, *"(1) For his own protection; (2) For the protection of the white Unionist; and (3) For the peace of the country. We put the musket in his hands because it was necessary; for the same reason we must*

Colonel Charles Dahnmon Whitt

give him the franchise." The support for voting rights was a compromise between moderate and radical Republicans.

The Republicans believed that the best way for men to get political experience was to be able to vote and to participate in the political system. They passed laws allowing all male freedmen to vote. In 1867, black men voted for the first time. Over the course of Reconstruction, more than 1,500 African Americans held public office in the South. They did not hold office in numbers representative of their proportion in the population, but often elected whites to represent them. The question of women's suffrage was also debated, but was rejected.

From 1890 to 1908, southern states passed new constitutions and laws that disfranchised tens of thousands of poor whites and many blacks with new voter registration and electoral rules.

Lincoln's Presidential Reconstruction

Confederate American

President Abraham Lincoln

16th President of the United States

1861-1865

Preliminary events

President Lincoln signed two Confiscation Acts into law, the first on August 6, 1861, and the second on July 17, 1862, safeguarding fugitive slaves from the Confederacy that came over into Union lines and giving them indirect emancipation if their masters continued insurrection against the United States. The laws allowed the confiscation of lands for colonization from those who aided and supported the rebellion. However, these laws

Colonel Charles Dahnmon Whitt

had limited effect as they were poorly funded by Congress and poorly enforced by Attorney General Edward Bates.

In August 1861, Maj. Gen. John C. Fremont, Union commander of the Western Department, declared martial law in Missouri, confiscated Confederate property, and emancipated their slaves. President Lincoln immediately ordered Fremont to rescind his emancipation declaration stating, *"I think there is great danger that . . . the liberating slaves of traitorous owners, will alarm our Southern Union friends, and turn them against us — perhaps ruin our fair prospect for Kentucky."* After Fremont refused to rescind the emancipation order, President Lincoln terminated him from active duty on November 2, 1861. Lincoln was concerned that border states would bolt from the Union if slaves were given their freedom. On May 26, 1862, Union Maj. Gen. David Hunter emancipated slaves in South Carolina, Georgia, and Florida stated all *"persons ... heretofore held as slaves ... forever free."* Lincoln, embarrassed by the order, rescinded Hunter's declaration and cancelled the emancipations.

On April 16, 1862 Lincoln signed a bill into law outlawing slavery in Washington D.C. and freeing the estimated 3,500 slaves in the city and on June 19, 1862 he signed legislation outlawing slavery in all U.S. territories. In July 1862, under the authority of the Confiscation Acts and an amended Force Bill of 1795, he authorized the recruitment of freed slaves into the Union army and seizure of any Confederate property for military purposes.

Gradual emancipation and compensation

In an effort to keep border states in the Union, President Lincoln as early as 1861 designed gradual compensated emancipation programs paid for by government bonds.

Confederate American

Lincoln desired Delaware, Maryland, Kentucky, and Missouri to *"adopt a system of gradual emancipation which should work the extinction of slavery in twenty years."* On March 26, 1862 Lincoln met with Senator Charles Sumner and recommended that a special joint session of Congress be conveyed to discuss giving financial aid to any border states who initiated a gradual emancipation plan. In April 1862, the joint session of Congress met, however, the border states were not interested and did not make any response to Lincoln or any Congressional emancipation proposal. Lincoln advocated compensated emancipation during the 1865 River Queen steamer conference.

Colonization (Bet you didn't know this!")

<u>In August 1862, President Lincoln met with African American leaders and urged them to colonize some place in Central America.</u> Lincoln planned to free the slaves in the Emancipation Proclamation and he was concerned that freedmen would not be well treated in the United States by whites both in the North and South. Although Lincoln gave assurances that the United States government would support and protect any colonies, the leaders declined the offer of colonization. Many free blacks had been opposed to colonization plans in the past and wanted to remain in the United States. President Lincoln persisted in his colonization plan believing that emancipation and colonization were part of the same program. Lincoln was successful by April, 1863 at sending black colonists to Haiti and 453 to Chiriqui in Central America; however, none of the colonies was able to remain self-sufficient. Frederick Douglas, a prominent 19th century American civil rights activist, criticized that

Colonel Charles Dahnmon Whitt

Lincoln was *"showing all his inconsistencies, his pride of race and blood, his contempt for Negroes and his canting hypocrisy."* Negros, according to Douglas, wanted citizen rights rather than to be colonized. By the end of 1863 President Lincoln gave up on African American colonization.

Military governors installed

Starting in March 1862, in an effort to forestall Reconstruction by the Radicals in Congress, President Lincoln installed military governors in certain rebellious states under Union military control. Although the states would not be recognized by the Radicals until an undetermined time, installation of military governors kept the administration of Reconstruction under Presidential control rather than that of the increasingly unsympathetic Radical Congress. On March 3, 1862, Lincoln installed a loyalist Democrat Senator Andrew Johnson, as Military Governor with the rank of Brigadier General in his home state of Tennessee. In May, 1862, Lincoln appointed Edward Stanly Military Governor of the coastal region of North Carolina with the rank of Brigadier General. Stanly resigned almost a year later when he angered Lincoln by closing two schools for black children in New Bern. After Lincoln installed Brigadier General George F. Sheply as Military Governor of Louisiana in May, 1862, Sheply sent two anti-slavery representatives, Benjamin Flanders and Michael Hahn, elected in December, 1862, to the House which capitulated and voted to seat them. In July, 1862, Lincoln installed Colonel John S. Phelps as Military Governor of Arkansas, though he resigned soon after due to poor health.

Confederate American

Emancipation Proclamation

In July 1862, President Lincoln became convinced that *"a military necessity"* was needed to strike at slavery in order to win the Civil War for the Union. The Confiscation Acts were only having a minimal effect to end slavery. On July 22, he wrote a first draft of the Emancipation Proclamation that freed the slaves in states in rebellion. Lincoln decided not to release the document until there was a Union victory in the battlefield. After he showed his cabinet the document, slight alterations were made in the wording. Then on September 22, 1862, George McClellan defeated Robert E. Lee at Antietam; the second draft of the Emancipation Proclamation was issued to the public the following day. On January 1, 1863, the second part of the Emancipation Proclamation was issued, specifically naming ten states in which slaves would be *"forever free"*. The proclamation did not name the states of Tennessee, Kentucky, Missouri, Maryland, and Delaware, and specifically excluded numerous counties in some other states. Eventually, as the Union Armies advanced into the Confederacy millions of slaves were set free. Many of these freedmen joined the Union army and fought in battles against the Confederate forces.

Louisiana plan

President Abraham Lincoln was concerned to effect a speedy restoration of the Confederate states to the Union after the Civil War. In 1863, President Lincoln proposed a moderate plan for the Reconstruction of the captured Confederate State of Louisiana. The plan granted amnesty to Rebels who took an oath of loyalty to the Union. Only 10% of the state's electorate had to take the

Colonel Charles Dahnmon Whitt

loyalty oath in order for the state to be readmitted into U.S. Congress. The state was required to abolish slavery in its new constitution. Identical Reconstruction plans would be adopted in Arkansas and Tennessee. By December 1864, the Lincoln plan of Reconstruction had been enacted in Louisiana and the legislature sent 2 Senators and 5 Representatives to take their seats in Washington. However, Congress refused to count any of the votes from Louisiana, Arkansas, and Tennessee, in essence rejecting Lincoln's moderate Reconstruction plan. Congress, at this time controlled by the Radicals, proposed the Wade-Davis Bill that required a majority of the state electorates to take the oath of loyalty to be admitted to Congress. Lincoln pocket-vetoed the bill and the rift widened between the moderates, who wanted to save the Union and win the war, and the Radicals, who wanted to effect a more complete change within Southern society.

Freedmen's Bureau

Main article: Freedmen's Bureau

On March 3, 1865, President Lincoln signed the Freedmen's Bureau Bill, a progressive piece of legislation sponsored by the Republicans to aid freedmen and white refugees. A federal Bureau was created to provide food, clothing, fuel, and advice on negotiating labor contracts. It attempted to oversee new relations between freedmen and their former masters. The Act, without deference to a person's color, authorized confiscated land to be leased for a period of three years and the ability t no more than 40 acres. The Bureau was to expire one year after the termination of the Civil War. Lincoln was assassinated before he could appoint a commissioner of the Bureau. A

Confederate American

popular myth was that the Act offered 40 acres and a mule.

Bans color discrimination

Other legislation was signed that broadened equality and rights for African Americans. Lincoln outlawed discrimination due to a person's color, in carrying U.S. mail, in riding on public street cars in Washington, and in pay for soldiers.

River Queen peace conference

At the urging of Lt. Gen. Ulysses S. Grant, President Abraham Lincoln, and Secretary of State William H. Seward met with three southern representatives to discuss the peaceful reconstruction of the Union and the Confederacy at a neutral location aboard the River Queen on February 3, 1865 in Hampton Roads, Virginia. The southern delegation included Confederate vice-president, Alexander H. Stephens, John A. Campbell, and Robert M.T. Hunter. The southerners proposed the Union recognition of the Confederacy, a joint Union-Confederate attack on Mexico to oust dictator Maximillian, and to allow an alternative subordinate status of servitude rather than slavery. Lincoln flatly denied recognition of the Confederacy and said that the slaves covered from his Emancipation Proclamation would not be reenslaved. The southerners were told that the Union States were about to pass the Thirteenth Amendment outlawing slavery. Lincoln urged the governor of Georgia to remove Confederate troops and *"ratify this Constitutional Amendment prospectively, so as to take effect, say in five years...Slavery is doomed."* Lincoln also urged

Colonel Charles Dahnmon Whitt

compensated emancipation for the slaves and believed that the North should be willing to share the costs of freedom. Although the meeting was cordial nothing became of the peace negotiations. A previous similar conference with Francis P. Blair, sent by Lincoln, and Jefferson Davis in Richmond on January 12, 1865 had also been unsuccessful.

Lincoln continued to advocate his Louisiana Plan as a model for all states up until his assassination on April 14, 1865. The plan successfully started the Reconstruction process of ratifying the Thirteenth Amendment in all states. Lincoln is typically portrayed as taking the moderate position and fighting the radical positions. There is considerable debate, had Lincoln lived, on how well he would have handled Congress during the Reconstruction process that took place after the Civil War ended. One historical camp argues that Lincoln's flexibility, pragmatism, and superior political skills with Congress would have solved Reconstruction with far less difficulty.

Confederate American

The other camp believes the radicals would have attempted to impeach Lincoln, just as they did to his

successor, Andrew Johnson, in 1868.

President Andrew Johnson 17th President of the United States

1865-1869

Northern anger over the assassination of Lincoln and the immense human cost of the war led to vengeful demands for harsh policies. Vice President Andrew Johnson had taken a hard line and spoke of hanging rebel Confederates, but when he succeeded Lincoln as President, Johnson took a much softer line, pardoning many Confederate leaders and former Confederates.

Colonel Charles Dahnmon Whitt

Jefferson Davis was held in prison for two years, but other Confederate leaders were not. There were no treason trials. Only one person, Captain Henry Wirz, the commandant of the prison camp in Andersonville, Georgia, was executed for war crimes.

Although resigned to the abolition of slavery, many former Confederates were not willing to accept the social changes nor political domination by former slaves. The defeated were unwilling to acknowledge that their society had changed. In the words of Benjamin F. Perry, President Johnson's choice as the provisional governor of South Carolina: *"First, the Negro is to be invested with all political power and then the antagonism of interest between capital and labor is to work out the result."*

The fears, however, of the mostly conservative planter elite and other leading white citizens were partly assuaged by the actions of President Johnson, who ensured that a wholesale land redistribution from the planters to the freedman did not occur. President Johnson ordered that confiscated or abandoned lands administered by the Freedman's Bureau would not be redistributed to the freedmen, but be returned to pardoned owners. Land was returned that would have been forfeited under the Confiscation Acts passed by Congress in 1861 and 1862.

Confederate American

Freedmen and the enactment of Black Codes

A Harper's Magazine political cartoon alleging Ku Klux Klan and White League opposition to Reconstruction

Southern state governments quickly enacted the restrictive *"black codes"*. However, they were abolished in 1866 and seldom had effect, because the Freedman's Bureau (not the local courts) handled the legal affairs of freedmen.

The Black Codes indicated the plans of the southern whites for the former slaves. The freedmen would have more rights than did free blacks before the war, but they still had only a limited set of second-class civil rights, no voting rights, and, since they were not citizens, they could not own firearms, serve on a jury in a lawsuit involving whites or move about without employment. The Black Codes would limit the black's ability to control their own

Colonel Charles Dahnmon Whitt

employment. The Black Codes outraged northern opinion. They were overthrown by the Civil Rights Act of 1866 that gave the freedmen full legal equality (except for the right to vote).

The freedmen rejected gang labor work patterns that had been used in slavery. With the strong backing of the Freedman's Bureau, they forced planters to bargain for their labor. Such bargaining soon led to the establishment of the system of sharecropping, which gave the freedmen greater economic independence and social autonomy than gang labor. However, because they lacked capital and the planters continued to own the means of production (tools, draft animals, and land), the freedmen were forced into producing cash crops (mainly cotton) for the land-owners and merchants, and they entered into a crop-lien system. Widespread poverty, disruption to an agricultural economy too dependent on cotton and the falling price of cotton, led within decades to the routine indebtedness of the majority of the freedmen, and poverty by many planters.

Northern officials gave varying reports on conditions for the freedmen in the South. One harsh assessment came from Carl Schurz, who reported on the situation in the states along the Gulf Coast. His report documented dozens of extra-judicial killings and claimed that hundreds or thousands more African Americans were killed.

The number of murders and assaults perpetrated upon Negroes is very great; we can form only an approximative estimate of what is going on in those parts of the South which are not closely garrisoned and from which no regular reports are received, by what occurs under the very eyes of our military authorities. As to my personal experience, I will only mention that during my two days

Confederate American

sojourn at Atlanta, one Negro was stabbed with fatal effect on the street, and three were poisoned, one of whom died. While I was at Montgomery, one Negro was cut across the throat evidently with intent to kill, and another was shot, but both escaped with their lives. Several papers attached to this report give an account of the number of capital cases that occurred at certain places during a certain period of time. It is a sad fact that the perpetration of those acts is not confined to that class of people which might be called the rabble. Carl Schurz, "Report on the Condition of the South", December 1865 (U.S. Senate Exec. Doc. No. 2, 39th Congress, 1st session).

The report included sworn testimony from soldiers and officials of the Freedman's Bureau. In Selma, Alabama, Major J.P. Houston noted that whites who killed 12 African Americans in his district never came to trial. Many more killings never became official cases. Captain Poillon described white patrols in southwestern Alabama *"who board some of the boats; after the boats leave they hang, shoot, or drown the victims they may find on them, and all those found on the roads or coming down the rivers are almost invariably murdered. The bewildered and terrified freedmen know not what to do, to leave is death; to remain is to suffer the increased burden imposed upon them by the cruel taskmaster, whose only interest is their labor, wrung from them by every device an inhuman ingenuity can devise; hence the lash and murder is resorted to intimidate those whom fear of an awful death alone cause to remain, while patrols, Negro dogs and spies, disguised as Yankees, keep constant guard over these unfortunate people."*

Colonel Charles Dahnmon Whitt

Moderate responses

During fall 1865, out of response to the Black codes and worrisome signs of Southern radicals, the Radical Republicans blocked the readmission of the former rebellious states to the Congress. Johnson, however, was content with allowing former Confederate states into the Union as long as their state governments adopted the 13th Amendment abolishing slavery. By December 6, 1865, the amendment was ratified and Johnson considered Reconstruction over. Johnson was following the moderate Lincoln Presidential Reconstruction policy to get the states readmitted as soon as possible.

Congress, however, controlled by the Radicals, had other plans. The Radicals were led by Charles Sumner in the Senate and Thaddeus Stevens in the House of Representatives. Congress, on December 4, 1865, rejected Johnson's moderate Presidential Reconstruction, and organized the Joint Committee on Reconstruction, a 15 member panel to devise stricter reconstruction requirements for the Southern states to be restored to the Union.

In January 1866, Congress also renewed the Freedman's Bureau, however, Johnson vetoed the Freedmen's Bureau Bill in February 1866. Although Johnson had sympathies for the plights of the freedmen he was against federal assistance. An attempt to override the veto failed on February 20, 1866. This veto shocked the Congressional Radicals. In response, both the Senate and House passed a joint resolution not to allow any Senator or Representative seat admittance until *Congress* decided when Reconstruction was finished.

Confederate American

Senator Lyman Trumbull of Illinois, leader of the moderate Republicans, took affront at the black codes. He proposed the first Civil Rights Law, because the abolition of slavery was empty if laws are to be enacted and enforced depriving persons of African descent of privileges which are essential to freemen... A law that does not allow a colored person to go from one county to another, and one that does not allow him to hold property, to teach, to preach, are certainly laws in violation of the rights of a freeman... The purpose of this bill is to destroy all these discriminations.

The key to the bill was the opening section:

> *All persons born in the United States ... are hereby declared to be citizens of the United States; and such citizens of every race and color, without regard to any previous condition of slavery ... shall have the same right in every State ...to make and enforce contracts, to sue, be parties, and give evidence, to inherit, purchase, lease, sell, hold, and convey real and personal property, and to full and equal benefit of all laws and proceedings for the security of person and property, as is enjoyed by white citizens, and shall be subject to like punishment, pains, and penalties and to none other, any law, statute, ordinance, regulation, or custom to the Contrary notwithstanding.*

Congress quickly passed the Civil Rights bill; the Senate on February 2 voted 33–12; the House on March 13 voted 111–38.

Colonel Charles Dahnmon Whitt
Johnson's vetoes to help the south will take him down.

Although strongly urged by moderates in Congress to sign the Civil Rights bill, Johnson broke decisively with them by vetoing it on March 27, 1866. His veto message objected to the measure because it conferred citizenship on the freedmen at a time when eleven out of thirty-six states were unrepresented and attempted to fix by Federal law *"a perfect equality of the white and black races in every State of the Union."* Johnson said it was an invasion by

Federal authority of the rights of the States. It had no warrant in the Constitution and was contrary to all precedents. It was a "stride toward centralization and the concentration of all legislative power in the national government."

Confederate American

The debate over reconstruction and the Freedman's Bureau was nationwide. This 1866 Pennsylvania election poster alleged that the Bureau kept the Negro in idleness at the expense of the hard working white taxpayer. A racist caricature of an African American is depicted. The Democratic Party, proclaiming itself the party of white men, north and south, supported Johnson. However the Republicans in Congress overrode his veto (the Senate by the close vote of 33:15, the House by 122:41) and the Civil Rights bill became law. Congress also passed a toned down Freedmen's Bureau Bill; Johnson quickly vetoed as he had done to the previous bill. This time, however, Congress had enough support and overrode Johnson's veto.

The last moderate proposal was the Fourteenth Amendment, whose principal drafter was Representative John Bingham. It was designed to put the key provisions of the Civil Rights Act into the Constitution, but it went much further. It extended citizenship to everyone born in the United States (except visitors and Indians on reservations) penalized states that did not give the vote to freedmen, and most importantly created new federal civil rights that could be protected by federal courts. It guaranteed the Federal war debt would be paid (and promised the Confederate debt would never be paid). Johnson used his influence to block the amendment in the states since three-fourths of the states were required for ratification (the amendment was later ratified.). The moderate effort to compromise with Johnson had failed and a political fight broke out between the Republicans (both Radical and moderate) on one side, and on the other side, Johnson and his allies in the Democratic party

Colonel Charles Dahnmon Whitt

in the North, and the conservative groupings (which used different names) in each southern state.

Congress imposes Radical Reconstruction

Republicans in Congress took control of Reconstruction policies after the election of 1866. Johnson ignored the policy mandate and he openly encouraged southern states to deny to ratify the 14th Amendment (except for Tennessee, all former confederate states did so, as did the border states of Delaware, Maryland and Kentucky). Radical Republicans in Congress, led by Stevens and Sumner, opened the way to suffrage for male freedmen. They were generally in control, although they had to compromise with the moderate Republicans (the Democrats in Congress had almost no power). Historians generally refer to this period as Radical Reconstruction.

The South's white leaders, who held power in the immediate postwar era before the vote was granted to the freedmen, renounced secession and slavery, but not white supremacy. People who had previously held power were angered in 1867 when new elections were held. New Republican lawmakers were elected by a coalition of white Unionists, freedmen and northerners who had settled in the South. Some leaders in the South tried to accommodate to new conditions.

Constitutional amendments

Three new Constitutional amendments, known as the Reconstruction Amendments, were adopted. The 13th Amendment abolished slavery and was ratified in 1865. The 14th Amendment was proposed in 1866 and ratified in 1868, guaranteeing United States citizenship to all persons born or naturalized in the United States *(except*

Confederate American

Native Americans), and granting them federal civil rights. The 15th Amendment, proposed in late February 1869 and passed in early February 1870, decreeing that the right to vote could not be denied because of "race, color, or previous condition of servitude". The amendment did not declare the vote an unconditional right and only prohibited these types of discrimination while specific electoral policies were deeply determined within each state. These amendments caused huge changes in the American social structure, and elevated the former slaves, freedmen, to equality with White citizens.

Statutes

Congress clarified the scope of the federal writ of habeas corpus to allow federal courts to vacate unlawful state court convictions or sentences in 1867 (28 U.S.C. §2254).

Military reconstruction

With the Radicals in control, Congress passed the Reconstruction Acts on July 19, 1867. The first Reconstruction Act placed ten Confederate states under military control, grouping them into five military districts:

- First Military District: Virginia, under General John Schofield
- Second Military District: The Carolinas, under General Daniel Sickles
- Third Military District: Georgia, Alabama and Florida, under General John Pope and George Meade
- Fourth Military District: Arkansas and Mississippi, under General Edward Ord

Colonel Charles Dahnmon Whitt

- Fifth Military District: Texas and Louisiana, under Generals Philip Sheridan and Winfield Scott Hancock

20,000 U.S troops were deployed to enforce the Act.

Tennessee was not made part of a military district (having already been readmitted to the Union) and therefore federal controls did not apply.

The ten Southern state governments were reconstituted under the direct control of the United States Army. One major purpose was to recognize and protect the right of African Americans to vote. There was little or no combat, but rather a state of martial law in which the military closely supervised local government, supervised elections, and tried to protect office holders and freedmen from violence. Blacks were enrolled as voters; former Confederate leaders were excluded for a limited period.[Foner 1988 p 274–5] No one state was entirely representative. Randolph Campbell describes what happened in Texas:

The first critical step was the registration of voters according to guidelines established by Congress and interpreted by Generals Sheridan and Charles Griffin. The Reconstruction Acts called for registering all adult males, white and black, except those who had ever sworn an oath to uphold the Constitution of the United States and then engaged in rebellion. General Sheridan interpreted these restrictions stringently, barring from registration not only all pre-1861 officials of state and local governments who had supported the Confederacy, but also all city officeholders and even minor functionaries such as sextons of cemeteries. In May Griffin ... appointed a three-man board of registrars for each county, making his

Confederate American

choices on the advice of known scalawags and local Freedman's Bureau agents. In every county where practicable a freedman served as one of the three registrars. Final registration amounted to approximately 59,633 whites and 49,479 blacks. It is impossible to say how many whites were rejected or refused to register (estimates vary from 7,500 to 12,000), but blacks, who constituted only about 30 percent of the state's population, were significantly overrepresented at 45 percent of all voters.

All Southern states were readmitted to representation in Congress by the end of 1870 the last being Georgia. All but 500 top Confederate leaders were pardoned when President Grant signed the Amnesty Act of 1872.

> General Grant released his Slaves after the 13th Admentment became law. Some folksa asked him why he held his slaves so long, he said, *"Good help is hard to get!"*
>
> This is the man that led the Union Army against the Confederacy. Do you think it was all about slavery?

Colonel Charles Dahnmon Whitt

Presidency of Ulysses S. Grant

Grant: the Radical President

President Ulysses S. Grant

18th President of the United States

Confederate American
1869-1877

During the Civil War, many in the North believed that fighting for the Union was a noble cause, for the preservation of liberty, equality, and democracy. After the war ended, with the North victorious, it was imperative to them to keep this commitment to liberty to honor all the Union soldiers, both black and white, those who had died in the many costly battles, those veterans who survived, as well as their families. The Radicals, who grew frustrated over President Andrew Johnson and ex-Confederates dismantling of Reconstruction laws, sought out a candidate for President who would uphold their legislation and who was committed to the Civil Rights of the freedmen.

In 1868, the Radicals unanimously chose Ulysses S. Grant to be the Republican Presidential candidate. Grant bolstered favor with the Radicals after he turned over the keys to the War Department, a move that allowed Edwin M. Stanton, a Radical, to be reinstated. As early as 1862, during the Civil War Grant had appointed the Ohio military chaplain John Eaton to protect and gradually incorporate refugee slaves in west Tennessee and northern Mississippi into the Union War effort and pay them for their labor. It was the beginning of his vision for the Freedmen's Bureau. Grant opposed President Andrew Johnson by supporting the Reconstruction Acts passed by Congress.

Grant would go on to serve two terms in office as the 18th President of the United States. He created the Department of Justice and Office of Solicitor General, led by Attorney General Amos Akerman and the first Solicitor

Colonel Charles Dahnmon Whitt

General Benjamin Bristow, who both prosecuted thousands of Klan's men under the Force Acts. Grant sent additional federal troops to nine South Carolina counties to suppress Klan violence in 1871. Grant also used military pressure to ensure that African Americans could maintain their new electoral status; endorsed the Fifteenth Amendment giving African Americans the right to vote and signed the Civil Rights Act of 1875 giving people access to public facilities regardless of race. Grant's support from Congress and the nation declined due to presidential scandals during his administration. As well as the political resurgence of the elite white planter class in the South based on the Democratic Party's use of paramilitary groups and the Republican Party's concern over financial monetary policies rather than protecting the freedmen.

Readmission to representation in Congress

- Tennessee – July 24, 1866
- Arkansas – June 22, 1868
- Florida – June 25, 1868
- North Carolina – July 4, 1868
- South Carolina – July 9, 1868
- Louisiana – July 9, 1868
- Alabama – July 13, 1868
- Virginia – January 26, 1870
- Mississippi – February 23, 1870
- Texas - March 30, 1870
- Georgia – July 15, 1870

African American officeholders

Republicans took control of all Southern state governorships and state legislatures, except for Virginia.

Confederate American

The Republican coalition elected numerous African-Americans to local, state, and national offices. About 137 black officeholders had lived outside the South before the Civil War. Some had escaped from slavery to the North and returned to help the South advance in the postwar era.

Many of them had achieved education and positions of leadership elsewhere. Other African American men who served were leaders in their communities, including a number of preachers. As happened in white communities, not all leadership depended upon wealth and literacy.

Carpetbaggers infest the South 1866.

Colonel Charles Dahnmon Whitt

First black senator elected.
Hiram Revels of Mississippi elected to U. S. Senate as the first black senator. 1866

Confederate American

There were few African Americans elected or appointed to national office. African Americans voted for white candidates and for blacks. The Fifteenth Amendment guaranteed the right to vote, but did not guarantee that the vote would be counted or the districts would be apportioned equally. As a result, even states with majority African American population often only had one or two African American representatives in Congress. Exceptions included South Carolina, which had four African Americans out of its five Congressmen at the end of Reconstruction.

Public schools

W. E. B. Du Bois argued that the freedmen had a deep commitment to education. African Americans in the Republican coalition played a critical role in establishing the principal of universal public education in state constitutions during congressional Reconstruction. Some slaves learned to read from white playmates although formal education was not allowed by law. African Americans started *"native schools"* before the end of the war. Sabbath schools were another widespread means freedmen created for teaching literacy. When they gained suffrage, black politicians took this commitment to public education to state constitutional conventions.

African Americans and white Republicans joined to build education at the state level. They created a system of public schools which were segregated by race everywhere except New Orleans. Generally, elementary and a few secondary schools were built in most cities, and occasionally in the countryside, but the South had few cities.

Colonel Charles Dahnmon Whitt

In the rural areas the public school was often a one-room affair that attracted about half the younger children. The teachers were poorly paid and their pay was often in arrears. Conservatives contended the rural schools were too expensive and unnecessary for a region where the vast majority of people were cotton or tobacco farmers. They had no vision of a better future for their residents. One historian found that the schools were less effective than they might have been because "poverty, the inability of the states to collect taxes, and inefficiency and corruption in many places prevented successful operation of the schools."

'TIS BUT A CHANGE OF BANNERS

Confederate American

1868 Republican cartoon identifies Democratic candidate Horatio Seymour with KKK violence and with Confederate soldiers

Numerous private academies and colleges for freedmen were established by northern missionaries. Every state created state colleges for freedmen, such as Alcorn State University in Mississippi. The state colleges created generations of teachers who were critical in the education of African American children.

In 1890, the black state colleges started receiving federal funds as land grant schools. They received state funds after Reconstruction ended because, as Lynch explains, "there are very many liberal, fair-minded and influential Democrats in the State who are strongly in favor of having the State provide for the liberal education of both races."

Railroad subsidies and payoffs.

Colonel Charles Dahnmon Whitt

Atlanta's railyard and roundhouse in ruins shortly after the end of the Civil War.

Every Southern state subsidized railroads, which modernizers felt could haul the South out of isolation and poverty. Millions of dollars in bonds and subsidies were fraudulently pocketed. One ring in North Carolina spent $200,000 in bribing the legislature and obtained millions in state money for its railroads. Instead of building new track, however, it used the funds to speculate in bonds, reward friends with extravagant fees and enjoy lavish trips to Europe. Taxes were quadrupled across the South to pay off the railroad bonds and the school costs. There were complaints among taxpayers, because taxes had historically been low, since there was so little commitment to public works or public education. Taxes historically had been much lower than in the North reflecting a lack of public investment in the communities. Nevertheless thousands of miles of lines were built as the Southern system expanded from 11,000 miles (17,700 km) in 1870 to 29,000 miles (46,700 km) in 1890. The lines were owned and directed overwhelmingly by Northerners. Railroads helped create a mechanically skilled group of craftsmen and broke the isolation of much of the region. Passengers were few, however, and apart from hauling the cotton crop when it was harvested, there was little freight traffic. As Franklin explains, "numerous railroads fed at the public trough by bribing legislators...and through the use and misuse of state funds." The effect, according to one businessman, "was to drive capital from the State, paralyze industry, and demoralize labor."

Taxation during Reconstruction

Confederate American

Reconstruction changed the tax structure of the South. In the U.S. from the earliest days until today, a major source of state revenue was the property tax. In the South, wealthy landowners were allowed to assess the value of their own land. These fraudulent assessments were almost valueless and pre-war property taxes collections were almost nothing. State revenues came from fees and from sales taxes on slave auctions. Some states assessed property owners by a combination of land value and a capitation tax, a tax on each worker employed. This tax was often assessed in a way to discourage a free labor market, where a slave was assessed at 75 cents, while a free white was assessed at a dollar or more, and a free African American at $3 or more. Some revenue also came from poll taxes. These taxes were more than poor people could pay, with the designed and inevitable consequence that they did not vote.

During Reconstruction, new spending on schools and infrastructure, combined with fraudulent spending and a collapse in state credit because of huge deficits, forced the states to dramatically increase property tax rates. In places, the rate went up to ten times higher, despite the poverty of the region. The infrastructure of much of the South, roads, bridges, and railroads, scarce and deficient even before the war had been destroyed during the war. In addition, there were other new expenditures, because pre-war southern states did not educate their citizens or build and maintain much infrastructure. In part, the new tax system was designed to force owners of large estates with huge tracts of uncultivated land either to sell or to have it confiscated for failure to pay taxes. The taxes would serve as a market-based system for redistributing the land to the landless freedmen and white poor.

Colonel Charles Dahnmon Whitt

Taxes were levied upon the landowners' own sworn testimony as to the value of their land which remained the dubious and exploitable system. Called upon to pay an actual tax on their property, angry plantation owners revolted. The conservatives shifted their focus away from race to taxes. Former Congressman John R. Lynch, a black Republican leader from Mississippi, concluded:

The argument made by the taxpayers, however, was plausible and it may be conceded that upon the whole they were about right; for no doubt it would have been much easier upon the taxpayers to have increased at that time the interest-bearing debt of the State than to have increased the tax rate. The latter course, however, had been adopted and could not then be changed.

Conservative reaction

The fact that their former slaves now held political and military power angered many whites. They self-consciously defended their own actions within the framework of an Anglo-American discourse of resistance against tyrannical government and they broadly succeeded in convincing fellow (white) citizens. They formed new political parties (often with "Conservative" in the title) to contest elections and supported or tolerated violent activist groups that intimidated both black and white Republican leaders at election time. By the mid 1870s, the Conservatives had aligned with the national Democratic Party, which enthusiastically supported their cause even as the national Republican Party was losing interest in Southern affairs. Historian Walter Lynwood Fleming describes mounting anger of Southern whites: *"The Negro troops, even at their best, were everywhere considered offensive by the native whites... The Negro soldier, impudent by reason of his new freedom, his new*

Confederate American

uniform, and his new gun, was more than Southern temper could tranquilly bear and race conflicts were frequent."

Most members of both the planter/business class and common farmer class of the South opposed black power, Carpetbaggers and military rule, and sought white supremacy. Democrats nominated blacks for political office and tried to steal other blacks from the Republican side. When these attempts to combine with the blacks failed, the planters joined the common farmers in simply trying to displace the Republican governments. The planters and their business allies dominated the selfstyled *"conservative coalition"* that finally took control in the South. They were paternalistic toward the blacks but feared they would use power to raise taxes and slow business development.

Fleming is a typical example of the conservative interpretation of Reconstruction. His work defended some roles in opposing military oppression by the white supremacist group the Ku Klux Klan, (KKK) but denounced the Klan's violence. Fleming accepted as necessary the disenfranchisement of African Americans because he thought their votes were bought and sold by Carpetbaggers. Fleming described the first results of the movement as "good" and the later ones as "both good and bad." According to Fleming (1907) the KKK "quieted the Negroes, made life and property safer, gave protection to women, stopped burnings, forced the radical leaders to be more moderate, made the Negroes work better, drove the worst of the Radical leaders from the country and started the whites on the way to gain political supremacy."

Colonel Charles Dahnmon Whitt

The evil result, Fleming said, was that lawless elements *"made use of the organization as a cloak to cover their misdeeds... the lynching habits of today [1907] are largely to conditions, social and legal, growing out of Reconstruction."*

Ellis Paxson Oberholtzer (a northern scholar) in 1917 explained: *"Outrages up on the poor and there were in plenty."* Their sufferings were many. But white men, too, were victims of lawless violence and in all portions of the North and the late "rebel" states. Not a political campaign passed without the exchange of bullets, the breaking of skulls with sticks and stones, the firing of rival clubhouses. Republican clubs marched the streets of Philadelphia, amid revolver shots and brickbats, to save the negroes from the *"rebel"* savages in Alabama... The project to make voters out of black men was not so much for their social elevation as for the further punishment of the Southern white people for the capture of offices for radical scamps and the entrenchment of the radical party in power for a long time to come in the South and in the country at large."

Reaction by the angry whites included the formation of violent secret societies, especially the KKK. Violence occurred in cities with Democrats, Conservatives and other angry whites on one side and Republicans, African-Americans, federal government representatives, and Republican-organized armed Loyal Leagues on the other. The victims of this violence were overwhelmingly African American. The Klan and other such groups were careful to avoid federal legal intervention or military conflict. Their election time tactics included violent intimidation of African American and Republican voters prior to elections while avoiding conflict with the U.S. Army or the state militias and then withdrawing completely on election day.

Confederate American

Conservative reaction continued in both the north and south. The *"white liners"* movement to elect candidates dedicated to white supremacy reached as far as Ohio in 1875.

Republicans split nationally: election of 1872

As early as 1868 Supreme Court Chief Justice Salmon P. Chase, a leading Radical during the war, concluded that:

"Congress was right in not limiting, by its reconstruction acts, the right of suffrage to whites; but wrong in the exclusion from suffrage of certain classes of citizens and all unable to take its prescribed retrospective oath, and wrong also in the establishment of despotic military governments for the States and in authorizing military commissions for the trial of civilians in time of peace. There should have been as little military government as possible; no military commissions; no classes excluded from suffrage; and no oath except one of faithful obedience and support to the Constitution and laws, and of sincere attachment to the constitutional Government of the United States."

By 1872, President Ulysses S. Grant had alienated large numbers of leading Republicans, including many radicals by the corruption of his administration and his use of federal soldiers to prop up radical state regimes in the South. The opponents, called *"Liberal Republicans"*, included founders of the party who expressed dismay that the party had succumbed to corruption. They were further wearied by the continued insurgent violence of whites against blacks in the South, especially around every election cycle, which demonstrated the war was not over

Colonel Charles Dahnmon Whitt

and changes were fragile. Leaders included editors of some of the nation's most powerful newspapers. Charles Sumner, embittered by the corruption of the Grant administration, joined the new party, which nominated editor Horace Greeley. The badly organized Democratic party also supported Greeley.

Grant made up for the defections by new gains among Union veterans and by strong support from the *"Stalwart"* faction of his party (which depended on his patronage), and the Southern Republican parties. Grant won a smashing landslide, as the Liberal Republican party vanished and many former supporters, even former abolitionists, abandoned the cause of Reconstruction.

Republican coalition splinters in South

In the South, political–racial tensions built up inside the Republican party as they were attacked by the Democrats. In 1868, Georgia Democrats, with support from some Republicans, expelled all 28 black Republican members, arguing blacks were eligible to vote, but not to hold office. In several states, the more conservative scalawags fought for control with the more radical carpetbaggers and usually lost. Thus, in Mississippi, the conservative faction led by scalawag James Lusk Alcorn was decisively defeated by the radical faction led by carpetbagger Adelbert Ames. The party lost support steadily as many scalawags left it; few recruits were acquired. Meanwhile, the freedmen were demanding a bigger share of the offices and patronage, thus squeezing out their carpetbagger allies. Finally some of the more prosperous freedmen were joining the Democrats, as they were angered at the failure of the Republicans to help them acquire land.

Confederate American

Although historians such as W. E. B. Du Bois looked for and celebrated a cross-racial coalition of poor whites and blacks, such coalitions rarely formed in these years. Writing in 1915, former Congressman Lynch, recalling his experience as a black leader in Mississippi.

He explained that; *"While the colored men did not look with favor upon a political alliance with the poor whites, it must be admitted that, with very few exceptions, that class of whites did not seek and did not seem to desire such an alliance."* Lynch reported that poor whites resented the job competition from freedmen. Furthermore, the poor whites with a few exceptions, were less efficient, less capable, and knew less about matters of state and governmental administration than many of the former slaves. As a rule, therefore, the whites that came into the leadership of the Republican party between 1872 and 1875 were representatives of the most substantial families of the land.

Democrats try a "New Departure"

Colonel Charles Dahnmon Whitt

Source: Thomas Nast
Last page: A political cartoon about the (Wheeler) Compromise in Louisiana
published in Harper's Weekly
March 6, 1875

A Republican Form of Government and No Domestic Violence

By 1870, the Democratic–Conservative leadership across the South decided it had to end its opposition to Reconstruction and black suffrage to survive and move on to new issues. The Grant administration had proven by its crackdown on the Ku Klux Klan that it would use as much federal power as necessary to suppress open anti-black violence. The Democrats in the North concurred. They wanted to fight the Republican Party on economic grounds rather than race. The New Departure offered the chance for a clean slate without having to refight the Civil War every election. Furthermore, many wealthy landowners thought they could control part of the newly enfranchised black electorate to their own advantage.

Not all Democrats agreed; an insurgent element continued to resist Reconstruction no matter what. Eventually, a group called *"Redeemers"* took control of the party in the Southern states. They formed coalitions with conservative Republicans, including scalawags and carpetbaggers, emphasizing the need for economic modernization. Railroad building was seen as a *cure all* since northern capital was needed. The new tactics were a success in Virginia where William Mahone built a winning coalition. In Tennessee, the Redeemers formed a coalition with Republican governor DeWitt Senter. Across the South some Democrats switched from the race issue to taxes and corruption, charging that Republican governments were corrupt and inefficient. With continuing decrease in cotton prices, taxes squeezed cash-poor farmers who rarely saw $20 in currency a year but had to pay taxes in currency or lose their farm.

In North Carolina, Republican Governor William Woods Holden used state troops against the Klan, but the prisoners were released by federal judges. Holden became the first governor in American history to be impeached and removed from office. Republican political disputes in Georgia split the party and enabled the Redeemers to take over.

Colonel Charles Dahnmon Whitt

In the lower South, violence continued and new insurgent groups arose. The disputed election in Louisiana in 1872 found both Republican and Democratic candidates holding inaugural balls while returns were reviewed. Both certified their own slates for local parish offices in many places, causing local tensions to rise. Finally, Federal support helped certify the Republican as governor, but the Democrat Samuel D. McEnery in March 1873 brought his own militia to bear in New Orleans, the seat of government.

Slates for local offices were certified by each candidate. In rural Grant Parish in the Red River Valley, freedmen fearing a Democratic attempt to take over the parish government reinforced defenses at the Colfax courthouse in late March. White militias gathered from the area a few miles outside the settlement. Rumors and fears abounded on both sides. William Ward, an African-American Union veteran and militia captain, mustered his company in Colfax and went to the courthouse. On Easter Sunday, April 13, 1873, the whites attacked the defenders at the courthouse. There was confusion about who shot one of the white leaders after an offer by the defenders to surrender. It was a catalyst to mayhem. In the end, three whites died and 120 to 150 blacks were killed, some 50 while held as prisoners. The disproportionate numbers of black to white fatalities and documentation of brutalized bodies are why contemporary historians call it the *Colfax Massacre* rather than the *Colfax Riot*, as it is known locally.

This marked the beginning of heightened insurgency and attacks on Republican officeholders and freedmen in Louisiana and other Deep South States. In Louisiana, on the way to court, Judge T.S. Crawford and District Attorney P.H. Harris of the 12th Judicial District were shot

Confederate American

off their horses and killed from ambush October 8, 1873. *One widow wrote to the Department of Justice that her husband was killed because he was a Union man and "...of the efforts made to screen those who committed a crime."* {US Senate Journal January 13, 1875, pp. 106–107}.

In the North, a live-and-let-live attitude made elections more like a sporting contest. But in the Deep South, many white citizens had not reconciled with the defeat of the war or the granting of citizenship to freedmen. As an Alabama scalawag explained,

Our contest here is for life, for the right to earn our bread...for a decent and respectful consideration as human beings and members of society.

Panic of 1873

The Panic of 1873 hit the Southern economy hard and disillusioned many Republicans who had gambled that railroads would pull the South out of its poverty. The price of cotton fell by half; many small landowners, local merchants and cotton factors (wholesalers) went bankrupt. Sharecropping for black and white farmers became more common as a way to spread the risk of owning land. The old abolitionist element in the North was aging away or had lost interest, and was not replenished. Many carpetbaggers returned to the North or joined the Redeemers. Blacks had an increased voice in the Republican Party, but across the South it was divided by internal bickering and was rapidly losing its cohesion. Many local black leaders started emphasizing individual economic progress in cooperation with white elites, rather

Colonel Charles Dahnmon Whitt

than racial political progress in opposition to them, a conservative attitude that foreshadowed Booker T. Washington.

Nationally, President Grant was blamed for the depression. The Republican Party lost 96 seats in all parts of the country in the 1874 elections. The Bourbon Democrats took control of the House and were confident of electing Samuel J. Tilden president in 1876. President Grant was not running for re-election and seemed to be losing interest in the South. States fell to the Redeemers, with only four in Republican hands in 1873, Arkansas, Louisiana, Mississippi and South Carolina; Arkansas then fell after the violent Brooks–Baxter War in 1874 ripped apart the Republican party there.

Paramilitary groups allied with Democratic Party

Political violence had been endemic in Louisiana, but in 1874 the white militias coalesced into paramilitary organizations such as the White League, first in parishes of the Red River Valley. A new organization operated openly and had political goals. The violent overthrow of Republican rule and suppression of black voting. White League chapters soon rose in many rural parishes receiving financing for advanced weaponry from wealthy men. In one example of local violence, the White League assassinated six white Republican officeholders and five to twenty black witnesses outside Coushatta, Red River Parish in 1874. Four of the white men were related to the Republican representative of the parish.

Later in 1874 the White League mounted a serious attempt to unseat the Republican governor of Louisiana, in a dispute that had simmered since the 1872 election. It brought 5000 troops to New Orleans to engage and

Confederate American

overwhelm forces of the Metropolitan Police and state militia to turn Republican Governor William P. Kellogg out of office and seat McEnery. The White League took over and held the state house and city hall, but they retreated before the arrival of reinforcing Federal troops. Kellogg had asked for reinforcements before and Grant finally responded, sending additional troops to try to quell violence throughout plantation areas of the Red River Valley, although 2,000 troops were already in the state.

Similarly, the Red Shirts, another paramilitary group, arose in 1875 in Mississippi and the Carolinas. Like the White League and White Liner rifle clubs these groups operated as a "military arm of the Democratic Party", to restore white supremacy.

Democrats and many northern Republicans agreed that Confederate nationalism and slavery were dead, the war goals were achieved and further federal military interference was an undemocratic violation of historic Republican values. The victory of Rutherford Hayes in the hotly contested Ohio gubernatorial election of 1875 indicated his "let alone" policy toward the South would become Republican policy, as happened when he won the 1876 Republican nomination for president.

An explosion of violence accompanied the campaign for the Mississippi's 1875 election, in which Red Shirts and Democratic rifle clubs, operating in the open and without disguise, threatened or shot enough Republicans to decide the election for the Democrats. Republican Governor Adelbert Ames asked Grant for federal troops to fight back. Grant initially refused, saying public opinion was *"tired out"* of the perpetual troubles in the South.

Colonel Charles Dahnmon Whitt

Ames fled the state as the Democrats took over Mississippi.

This was not the end of the violence, however, as the campaigns and elections of 1876 were marked by additional murders and attacks on Republicans in Louisiana, North Carolina, South Carolina, and Florida. In South Carolina the campaign season of 1876 was marked by murderous outbreaks and fraud against freedmen. Red Shirts paraded with arms behind Democratic candidates; they killed blacks in the Hamburg and Ellenton SC massacres; and one historian estimated 150 blacks were killed in the weeks before the 1876 election across South Carolina. Red Shirts prevented almost all black voting in two majority-black counties. The Red Shirts were also active in North Carolina.

Election of 1876

Reconstruction continued in South Carolina, Louisiana and Florida until 1877. The elections of 1876 were accompanied by heightened violence across the Deep South. A combination of ballot stuffing and intimidating blacks suppressed their vote even in majority black counties. The White League was active in Louisiana. After Republican Rutherford Hayes won the disputed U.S. Presidential election of 1876, the national Compromise of 1877 was reached.

The white Democrats in the South agreed to accept Hayes' victory if he withdrew the last Federal troops. By this point, the North was weary of insurgency. White Democrats controlled most of the Southern legislatures and armed militias controlled small towns and rural areas. They considered Reconstruction a failure because the

Confederate American

Federal government withdrew from enforcing their ability to exercise their rights as citizens.

Hayes: the last Reconstruction President

President Rutherford B. Hayes

19th President of the United States

1877-1881

Colonel Charles Dahnmon Whitt

On January 29, 1877 President Ulysses S. Grant signed the Electoral Commission Act that set up a 15 member commission to settle the dis Electoral Commission awarded Rutherford B. Hayes the electoral votes he needed; Congress certified he had won by one electoral vote. The Democrats had little leverage, they could not block Hayes' election, but they were mollified by the implicit, "back room" deal that federal troops would be removed on the condition that the Southern states pledged to protect the lives of African Americans. Hayes' friends also let it be known that he would promote federal aid for internal improvements and name a Southerner to his cabinet and help a railroad in Texas. With the removal of Northern troops the President had no method to enforce Reconstruction thus this *"back room"* deal signaled the end of American Reconstruction.

After assuming office on March 4, 1877, President Hayes removed troops from the capitols of the remaining Reconstruction states, Louisiana and South Carolina, allowing the Redeemers to have full control of these states. President Grant had already removed troops from Florida, before Hayes was inaugurated, and troops from the other Reconstruction states had long since been withdrawn. Hayes also appointed David M. Key from Tennessee, a Southern Democrat, to the position of Postmaster General. By 1879, thousands of African American "exodusters" packed up and headed to new opportunities in Kansas. The Democrats gained control of the Senate and now had complete control of Congress having already taken over the House in 1875. Hayes vetoed bills from the Democrats that outlawed the Republican Force Acts, however, with the military underfunded, Hayes could not adequately enforce these laws. Blacks remained involved in Southern politics,

Confederate American

particularly in Virginia, which was run by the biracial Readjuster Party.

The interpretation of Reconstruction has swung back and forth several times. Nearly all historians hold that Reconstruction ended in failure. It is hard to see Reconstruction "as concluding in anything but failure" says Etcheson (2009) Etcheson adds, "W. E. B. DuBois captured that failure well when he wrote in *Black Reconstruction in America* (1935): 'The slave went free; stood a brief moment in the sun; then moved back again toward slavery.'" Likewise Eric Foner concludes that from the black point of view, *"Reconstruction must be judged a failure."* The many factors contributing to this failure include: lack of a permanent federal agency *specifically* designed for the enforcement of civil rights; the Morrison R. Waite Supreme Court decisions that dismantled previous congressional civil rights legislation; and the economic reestablishment of conservative white planters in the South by 1877. Historian William McFeely explained that although the Constitutional amendments and civil rights legislation on their own merit were remarkable achievements no permanent government agency whose specific purpose was civil rights enforcement had been created.

The first generation of Northern historians believed that the former Confederates were traitors and Johnson was their ally who threatened to undo the Union's Constitutional achievements. By the 1880s, however, Northern historians argued that Johnson and his allies were not traitors but blundered badly in rejecting the 14th Amendment and setting the stage for Radical Reconstruction.

Colonel Charles Dahnmon Whitt

The black leader Booker T. Washington, who grew up in West Virginia during Reconstruction, concluded that, "the Reconstruction experiment in racial democracy failed because it began at the wrong end, emphasizing political means and civil rights acts rather than economic means and self-determination." His solution was to concentrate on building the economic infrastructure of the black community, in part by his leadership of Tuskegee Institute.

In popular literature two novels by Thomas Dixon, *The Clansman* (1905) and *The Leopard's Spots: A Romance of the White Man's Burden, 1865 to 1900* (1902), romanticized white resistance to Northern/black coercion, hailing vigilante action by the KKK. Other authors romanticized the benevolence of slavery and the happy world of the antebellum plantation. These sentiments were expressed on the screen in D.W. Griffith's anti-Republican 1915 movie *The Birth of a Nation*.

The Dunning School of scholars based at the history department of Columbia University analyzed Reconstruction as a failure, at least after 1866, for different reasons. They claimed that it took freedoms and rights from qualified whites and gave them to unqualified blacks who were being duped by corrupt carpetbaggers and scalawags. As one scholar notes, "Reconstruction was a battle between two extremes: the Democrats, as the group which included the vast majority of the whites, standing for decent government and racial supremacy, versus the Republicans, the Negroes, alien carpetbaggers, and renegade scalawags, standing for dishonest government and alien ideals. These historians wrote literally in terms of white and black."

In the 1930s *revisionism* became popular among scholars. As disciples of Charles A. Beard, revisionists

Confederate American

focused on economics, downplaying politics and constitutional issues. They argued that the radical rhetoric of equal rights was mostly a smokescreen hiding the true motivation of Reconstruction's real backers. Howard K. Beale argued Reconstruction was primarily a successful attempt by financiers, railroad builders and industrialists in the Northeast, using the Republican Party, to control the national government for their own selfish economic ends. Those ends were to continue the wartime high protective tariff, the new network of national banks and to guarantee a *sound* currency. To succeed the business class had to remove the old ruling agrarian class of Southern planters and Midwestern farmers. This it did by inaugurating Reconstruction, which made the South Republican, and by selling its policies to the voters wrapped up in such attractive vote-getting packages as Northern patriotism or the bloody shirt. Historian William Hesseltine added the point that the Northeastern businessmen wanted to control the South economically, which they did through ownership of the railroads. However, historians in the 1950s and 1960s refuted Beale's economic causation by demonstrating that Northern businessmen were widely divergent on monetary or tariff policy and seldom paid attention to Reconstruction issues.

The black scholar W. E. B. Du Bois, in his *Black Reconstruction in America, 1860–1880*, published in 1935, compared results across the states to show achievements by the Reconstruction legislatures and to refute claims about wholesale African-American control of governments. He showed black contributions, as in the establishment of universal public education, charitable and social institutions and universal suffrage as important results and he noted their collaboration with whites. He

Colonel Charles Dahnmon Whitt

also pointed out that whites benefited most by the financial deals made and he put excesses in the perspective of the war's aftermath. He noted that despite complaints several states kept their Reconstruction constitutions for nearly a quarter of a century. Despite receiving favorable reviews his work was largely ignored by white historians.

In the 1960s neoabolitionist historians emerged, led by John Hope Franklin, Kenneth Stampp, and Eric Foner. Influenced by the Civil Rights Movement they rejected the Dunning school and found a great deal to praise in Radical Reconstruction. Foner, the primary advocate of this view, argued that it was never truly completed, and that a Second Reconstruction was needed in the late 20th century to complete the goal of full equality for African Americans. The neo-abolitionists followed the revisionists in minimizing the corruption and waste created by Republican state governments, saying it was no worse than Boss Tweed's ring in New York City.

Instead they emphasized that suppression of the rights of African Americans was a worse scandal and a grave corruption of America's republican ideals. They argued that the tragedy of Reconstruction was not that it failed because blacks were incapable of governing, especially as they did not dominate any state government, but that it failed because whites raised an insurgent movement to restore white supremacy. White elite-dominated state legislatures passed disfranchising constitutions from 1890 to 1908 that effectively barred most blacks and many poor whites from voting. This disfranchisement affected millions of people for decades into the 20th century and closed African Americans and poor whites out of the political process in the South.

Confederate American

Reestablishment of white supremacy meant that within a decade people forgot that blacks were creating thriving middle classes in many states of the South. African Americans' lack of representation meant they were treated as second-class citizens, with schools and services consistently underfunded in segregated societies, no representation on juries or in law enforcement, and bias in other legislation. It was not until the Civil Rights Movement and the passage of Federal legislation that African Americans regained their sufferage and civil rights in the South under what is sometimes referred to as the *"Second Reconstruction."*

More recent work by Nina Silber, David W. Blight, Cecelia O'Leary, Laura Edwards, LeeAnn Whites and Edward J. Blum, has encouraged greater attention to race, religion and issues of gender while at the same time pushing the *end* of Reconstruction to the end of the 19th century, while monographs by Charles Reagan Wilson, Gaines Foster, W. Scott Poole and Bruce Baker have offered new views of the Southern "Lost Cause".

While 1877 is the usual date given for the end of Reconstruction, some historians extend the era to the 1890s. Reconstruction is unanimously considered a failure, though the reason for this is a matter of controversy.

- *The Dunning School considered failure inevitable because they felt that taking the power away from Southern whites was a violation of republicanism.*
- *A second school sees the reason for failure as Northern Republicans' lack of effectiveness in guaranteeing political rights to blacks.*

Colonel Charles Dahnmon Whitt

- *A third school blames the failure of not giving land to the freedmen so they could have their own economic base of power.*
- *A fourth school sees the major reason for failure of reconstruction as the states' inability to suppress the violence of Southern whites when they sought reversal for blacks' gains. Etcheson (2009) points to the "violence that crushed black aspirations and the abandonment by Northern whites of Southern Republicans."*

Reconstruction state-by-state – significant dates

Reconstruction in each State Declared Secession:

Joined Confederacy,

Readmitted to Congress,

Democratic Party Establishes Control

South Carolina December 20, 1860 February 4, 1861 July 9, 1868, April 11, 1877

Mississippi January 9, 1861 February 4, 1861 February 23, 1870, January 4, 1876

Florida January 10, 1861 February 4, 1861 June 25, 1868, January 2, 1877

Alabama January 11, 1861 February 4, 1861 July 14, 1868, November 16, 1874

Georgia January 19, 1861 February 4, 1861 July 15, 1870, November 1, 1871

Louisiana January 26, 1861 February 4, 1861 June 25 or July 9, 1868 January 2, 1877

Texas February 1, 1861 March 2, 1861 March 30, 1870, January 14, 1873

Confederate American

Virginia April 17, 1861 May 7, 1861 January 26, 1870, October 5, 1869

Arkansas May 6, 1861 May 18, 1861 June 22, 1868, November 10, 1874

North Carolina May 21, 1861 May 16, 1861 July 4, 1868, **November 28, 1870**

Tennessee June 8, 1861 May 16, 1861 July 24, 1866, October 4, 1869

RECONSTRUCTION!!
Source: Confederate Military History, Volume 12

A southern Point of View!

What is known as the reconstruction of the seceded states is a very sad tale to recall and no American who loves his country likes to bring back its harsh memories. Yet it is a matter of history and it needs be recorded in order that the part which the North and the South played during that period should be fully understood. It began under President Lincoln before the close of the war and was carried on by President Johnson after the assassination of President Lincoln, during the years 1865 and 1866. Afterward there was a second phase of reconstruction, or *"destruction,"* known as the congressional plan which undid all that had been done by Presidents Lincoln and Johnson. This latter period was the greatest trial that the South had to bear, not excepting the terrible ordeal of war. To understand properly the surroundings, it is necessary to enumerate briefly the events which occurred early in 1865, and the directions given by President Johnson to the military officers of the United States. First, I would mention the death of Mr. Lincoln himself, which was regarded as the greatest calamity that could have happened to the people of the

Colonel Charles Dahnmon Whitt

South. The arrest and imprisonment of President Davis and many of the Confederate soldiers and statesmen have been already related. The treatment of Mr. Davis was very harsh indeed, complicity in the assassination of Mr. Lincoln being cruelly imputed to him, and a large reward offered for his capture. He was placed in prison and shackled with irons in the strongest fortress in the Union, and a military guard placed over him day and night. Every town, village and district was occupied rapidly by the Union troops as the Confederate resistance melted away, and all civil government was ignored. The governors of most of the seceded States attempted to call their legislatures together to conform to the results of the war and take steps for their restoration to the Union. They did this, believing that the American principle of government, the sovereignty and indestructibility of the States, would be respected and that these prompt proceedings would be favored as the constitutional plan of restoration. They did this also believing it absolutely necessary to preserve civil government, and to show by legislative enactment complete submission to the results of the war in repealing their ordinances of secession and in accepting the freedom of the Negro.

The order issued by General Wilson, of the United States army in Georgia, when the legislature was called to meet, was to this effect: *"Neither the legislature nor any other political body will be permitted to assemble under the call of the rebel State authorities."* The spirit of this order was carried out in all the seceded States. Existing civil government was ignored everywhere and military rule inaugurated in municipal and local communities. The only government allowed was that of the local military officers, or under their supervision.

Confederate American

This harsh action of the United States authorities, civil and military, immediately following the collapse of the Confederate government, caused all prominent actors in the war to feel insecure. They did not know what to expect. It was not known how general the arrests and imprisonments would be and many leading men, civil and military, escaped to foreign lands, and for the time expatriated themselves. Gen. Jubal Early, with others, escaped to Cuba. Generals Loring, Graves, and a few other officers went to Egypt and took service under the authority of, Hons. Robert Toombs, J. C. Breckinridge and many others went to Europe. Gov. Isham G. Harris, Generals J. Bankhead Magruder, Hindman and Price went to Mexico; in fact, prominent citizens and soldiers everywhere felt great apprehension as to the course of the government even with their paroles. It was even contemplated by President Johnson and his advisers to arrest and imprison Gen. Robert E. Lee, who had surrendered his army to General Grant and had been paroled. General Grant, however, entered a vigorous protest against such action and insisted that men who had surrendered with arms in their hands were entitled to the usual laws recognized by all civilized nations and that their paroles should be respected. This action on his part and the advice of Gen. Robert E. Lee and the leading statesmen, officers and soldiers of all the lately seceded States, caused it to be thought best for all to remain in their respective States and share whatever fate was in store for the South. The feeling of expatriation was greatly allayed when such prominent men advised against it.

Colonel Charles Dahnmon Whitt
Colonel Charles Dahnmon Whitt

Colonel Whitt is a native of Tazewell County Virginia, but has lived in Greenup County for forty years. He loves regional history, Civil War History, and genealogy.

With this love pushing him he has become a researcher, genealogist, and a novelist. In the last decade the Colonel has dug up an enormous amount of genealogy data and now keeps a web site with over 15,600 names to search and over 300 pictures to look at.

The Colonel especially loves reenactments of the War Between the States. Even though many people think that war was fought over slavery, the Colonel has determined that slavery was brought to the forefront to gain support of the Northern Citizens. The Colonel has found that only 2% of the Confederate Soldiers owned slaves and General Grant's wife owned slaves while he led the northern armies invading the South.

With Genealogy the Colonel found his G G Grand Fathers Grave in Greenup County after living in the county for thirty years. This genealogy data has led to two books. "Legacy, The Days of David Crockett Whitt," which is the story of the Colonel's Great Grandfather. This 580 page book covers the years of 1836 to 1900 and is historic-fiction.

Confederate American

The Colonel keeps the dates, names, and places correct while letting the characters live out their lives in a harder, but simpler age. The Colonel has inserted Christian witness through out the book in prayers, and bits of scripture from the Holy Bible.

The Colonel's last effort to present is called "The Patriot, Hezekiah Whitt," which is the Colonel's GGG Grand Father. This work deals with the years of 1760 to 1846. Indian stories abound as these hardy people build America. It is also based on a true story, but is written in the historic-fiction fashion.

The Colonel was pleased to add a few bits to the Historic Book about Greenup County.

For more Information about the Colonel you may go to his web site at
http://dahnmonwhittfamily.com

I love my Tazewell County, Virginia and Kentucky especially my Greenup County.

Colonel Charles Dahnmon Whitt

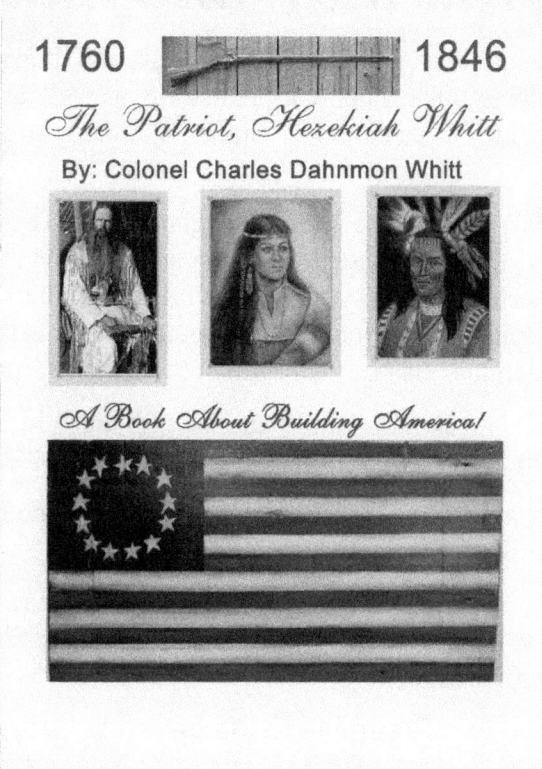

The Building Of America Series

MY other book, "The Patriot, Hezekiah Whitt"

This is a story about a great man, A Patriot to the Free State of Virginia; Hezekiah Whitt lived from 1761 to 1846. We will go to many places and have many adventures.

Hezekiah Whitt will find a beautiful land while scouting for Indians. This place is in present day Tazewell County, Virginia on the "Waters of the Clinch." It would become his beloved home for many years.

Confederate American

I will be as accurate as possible, but I will use my thoughts to fill in the missing links. This will be historic, as well as fictional. I will try to keep names, places, and dates as accurate as possible.

Hezekiah was a rebel to the King of England, but a Patriot to his home country, the Free State of Virginia and the new United States of America.   Will you travel with Hezekiah as he goes on campaigns against the Indians, Tories, and spies out the Indians and defends his liberties against the King of England?

You will meet Hezekiah's family and be with the Whitts as they make a life on the "Waters of the Clinch."

Indian stories abound as Hezekiah becomes a prominent man in the new County of Tazewell, Virginia.

Indiana, Illinois, Ohio, Kentucky, Tennessee, Missouri, Virginia, what is now West Virginia and Canada are all mentioned in this collection.

This Narrative is a Preamble to the book, "Legacy, The Days of David Crockett Whitt.". These two books are a series on "The Building of America."
           INDIAN STORIES ABOUND!
Go to http://dahnmonwhittfamily.com for more information on "Legacy, The Days Of David Crockett Whitt" Also see and order at: www.jsfbooks.com and Amazon.com
This Narrative is based on the life of Hezekiah Whitt, his Indian wife Rachel Cornstalk Skaggs Whitt
The price for this large 10 x 7 hardback is $30. Plus $6. for priority mail shipping.
For a personal Signed Copy, send check to Charles Whitt, P.O. Box 831, Flatwoods, KY. 41139 or **go to my site** http://dahnmonwhittfamily.com **and just click and put in your credit card info. You will still get a signed copy.**
E-Mail for questions.   C-dahnmon@roadrunner.com

Colonel Charles Dahnmon Whitt

Colonel Charles Dahnmon Whitt

I hope this book has spread some new light on the Confederates and why they tried to defend their homeland for four long bloody years.
<u>Confederate</u> <u>is not a "Dirty Word."</u>

Confederate American

The Southern people suffered greatly in the war and the next forty years after the war.

Today many in the north and in the south have a better understanding of the war, even though it is taught in schools that it was all about slavery.

In 1860 the Confederacy would have been ranked as the fourth richest country of the world. In four bloody years it was gone with the *"North Wind."*

Colonel Charles Dahnmon Whitt

Other Books by the Colonel:

"Legacy, The Days of David Crockett Whitt"

"Dahnmon's Little Stories"

"The Patriot, Hezekiah Whitt"

"Haunts and Spirits of the Past"

E-books are on Amazon.com Kindle if you want to pay less and just read!

www.ingramcontent.com/pod-product-compliance
Lightning Source LLC
Chambersburg PA
CBHW031617160426
43196CB00006B/173